THE COST OF THE BADGE:

LESSONS ON SERVICE, SACRIFICE AND SURVIVAL

WRITTEN BY

BRENT BEHRENS

THE COST OF THE BADGE: LESSONS ON SERVICE, SACRIFICE, AND SURVIVAL

This book is a work of nonfiction. The views and opinions expressed are those of the author and do not necessarily reflect the official policy or position of any agency, employer, or organization. Names, identifying details, and events have been altered where necessary to protect privacy and confidentiality.

This publication is intended for informational and educational purposes only and does not constitute legal, medical, or professional advice. The author and publisher disclaim any liability arising from the use or misuse of the information contained herein.

First Edition

Library of Congress Control Number: 2026909159

ISBN: 979-8-9956318-0-4

Published by Bear Parchment Press

BEAR PARCHMENT

PRESS

Table of Contents

The Cost of the Badge.. 1

"A Real Problem" 7

Perspective.. 13

Knowledge over Arrogance... 20

Seeing is Believing.. 31

What Goes Up Will Come down.. 37

You Knew... 43

Train Like It Matters.. 53

The School Skipper... 65

Car or Coffin.. 73

Is Somebody Watching?.. 80

Earn Your Edge... 86

The Barking Chicken.. 92

Down Range... 98

You're Never Out of the Fight.. 113

Conclusion... 118

I

The Cost of the Badge

At first glance, a badge appears to be nothing more than a piece of silver or gold-colored metal. In reality, its true cost has never been measured in metal. The cost of the badge is paid in sacrifice. Sometimes in small, unseen ways and sometimes at the highest price imaginable.

Across the United States, men and women have paid for that badge with far more than money. Some have paid with years away from their families, with sleepless nights, and with missed milestones. Others have paid with their lives. You may wonder why anyone would be willing to make such a sacrifice for something so small and unassuming. If you find yourself asking that question, you will never know the answer.

In 2025 alone, 104 men and women gave their lives in service to the badge. In 2024, that number was 170. In a nation of approximately 340 million people, these losses represent only a tiny fraction of the population. To some, that percentage may seem insignificant or even nonexistent. But to the families who live with that loss, the number means everything. It represents empty seats at dinner tables, unfinished conversations, children who will grow up without a mother or father, and lives permanently altered. This is the true cost of the badge.

A line-of-duty death is the unimaginable loss of a hero. That loss reaches far beyond family and close friends. It ripples throughout entire communities. I have personally witnessed countless members of the public step forward to share stories about law enforcement officers who changed their lives in ways both large and small. These stories reveal the quiet and lasting impact of service, an impact that often goes unnoticed until it is suddenly gone.

The harsh reality is that time moves on. The uniform is eventually worn by someone new. The seat in the briefing room is filled again. The department continues forward because it must. In that forward motion, the fallen are often remembered only once a year, on the anniversary of their death or during an annual memorial service.

What remains is the space they once occupied, the lives they touched, and the sacrifice that can never truly be replaced. Why would a man or woman willingly put on a badge, a duty belt, a ballistic vest, and lace up their boots knowing that each shift may demand their life, in exchange for someone else's?

Is it a death wish? A test of fate? Or is it the familiar phrase we have all heard: I want to make a difference in my community. Perhaps, for some, it is the pursuit of recognition, the image, the status, or the fleeting approval found on social media. Or perhaps it is something far quieter and deeper: a calling formed long before adulthood, a dream rooted in childhood, shaped by values, mentors, and moments that left lasting impressions.

The truth is that there is no single answer. The reason cannot be explained from the outside. It can only be understood by the person who chooses, day after day, to put on the badge. All too often, harsh judgments are handed down by the public, by municipal and county governments, and even by celebrities with far-reaching voices. Opinions are formed quickly, spoken loudly, and rarely tempered by experience. What many of these critics share is a common distance from the reality they judge.

They have never shouldered the badge themselves. They have never stood in the uncertainty, accepted the risks that come with protecting others, or discovered what the badge actually costs. It is easy to pass judgment from a place of safety or wealth. It is easy to critique sacrifice when you have never been asked to make one. It is precisely this distance, the gap between observation and experience, that obscures the true nature of bravery.

Bravery is not bought. Bravery is not given. Bravery comes from within. It is not found behind a desk or hidden behind diplomatic immunity, foreign or domestic. The cost of the badge does not end with death, nor does it begin with heroism. It lives in the quiet spaces in between. It lives in the constant vigilance that never truly shuts off in the way an officer scans a room without thinking, notices hands before faces, and listens differently to silence.

It lives in the accumulated weight of decisions that had no perfect outcome, only the least damaging one. This cost is invisible to most people, but it shapes how officers move through the world long after the shift ends. It is paid in relationships strained by both absence and presence. It is paid when an officer comes home physically present but mentally elsewhere, still carrying the weight of another family's worst moment. It is paid when spouses learn to read tone instead of words, when children learn not to ask certain questions, and when laughter at the dinner table briefly masks the truth that tomorrow is never guaranteed. These are not dramatic sacrifices. They are persistent ones, and they compound quietly over time.

The badge also demands a moral cost. Officers must act with authority while exercising restraint. They must be decisive without becoming cruel, and absorb anger without returning it. They are expected to show compassion to people who may show them none, remain calm in environments designed to provoke fear, and make irreversible decisions in seconds that will be debated in courtrooms and offices for years.

This is not a burden most people are ever asked to carry. Yet it is one officers shoulder routinely, often without acknowledgment. Perspective earned through exposure to real problems creates distance not because officers believe themselves above others, but because their internal scale has changed. What unsettles the public may barely register anymore, and what truly matters becomes difficult to explain without sounding detached or dismissive.

This gap widens over time, leaving many officers feeling misunderstood even by those closest to them. It is a lonely consequence of experience, rarely discussed but deeply felt. Still, despite the cost, the risk, and the certainty that the badge will take more than it gives, men and women continue to choose it. They continue not because they are unaware of the danger, but because they accept it.

They understand that the badge is not a symbol of power. It is a symbol of responsibility. Its weight is not felt on the chest, but carried in the mind and heart. The cost of the badge is real, enduring, and often unpaid in gratitude. Yet for those who wear it with intention, it remains worth bearing not for recognition, but for the quiet knowledge that when a real problem appears, someone must be willing to stand in its path.

II

"A Real Problem"

Merriam-Webster defines a problem as "a question raised for inquiry, consideration, or solution," or "a source of perplexity, distress, or vexation." By that definition, almost anything can be labeled a problem. Yet the true weight of a problem is often misunderstood, much like the cost of the badge itself.

I have watched people overwhelmed by minor inconveniences lash out at others or allow stress to dictate their behavior. In those moments, I have often responded with a blunt truth: "This is not a problem. There is no reason to act this way or treat people this way. You have never dealt with a real problem in your life."

The words sound harsh, and they are rarely received well. In reality, truth and harshness often travel together. There is a difference between inconvenience, adversity, and frustration, as opposed to a genuine crisis or a real problem. Recognizing that difference is uncomfortable, but it is necessary to understand the mindset of someone who has experienced a true crisis.

One of the first real problems I ever encountered began with a dispatch call to the home of a fifty-four-year-old man who had been found unresponsive by his twenty-seven-year-old daughter. Until that moment, before arriving at that house, I believed my life had already been filled with real problems. I learned very quickly that I was mistaken.

As I approached the residence, a wave of fear washed over me. Questions flooded my mind. Would I remember how to perform CPR correctly? Would I remember how to properly use my AED? What had happened before we arrived that caused this man to become unresponsive? Was this a genuine emergency or was it an ambush designed to lure my partner and me inside?

The walk from the driveway to the front door felt like a lifetime, even though it lasted only seconds. As we approached the door, it suddenly flew open. A young woman stood there, visibly distraught, tears rolling down her face as she sobbed uncontrollably and pointed toward a back bedroom. My thoughts raced. What is going on? Where is this unresponsive person? Is there anyone else in the house?

In that moment, I believed I was facing a real problem because of the uncertainty and the fear that I might not be prepared. I rushed into the bedroom and saw a white male of slender build with medium-length gray hair lying on his back. He was completely unclothed. His upper body was inside the bedroom while his lower body extended into the entrance of the bathroom.

I placed my equipment on the floor beside him and began performing CPR. The moment I touched him, I knew. His body was ice cold and rigid. His eyes were fixed open, and a faint haze clouded their blue color. In that instant, I knew he was dead. Panic set in, and I looked toward my partner, my field training officer, and asked the only question I could think of:

"What do I do?"

Unfazed, he looked at me and answered calmly and honestly.

"There's nothing we can do; he's dead."

That was the beginning of my first real problem.

In that moment, a flood of emotion rushed through me. What am I supposed to do? How do I fix this? How do I make this better? Every instinct in me wanted to act, to solve the situation, to undo what had already happened. The harsh truth quickly settled in: my partner was right. There was nothing we could do. The man's daughter rushed into the room, screaming and pleading with my partner and me to save her father. I stood up, walked toward her, and said the words no one should ever have to hear.

"Ma'am, your father is dead. Unfortunately, there is nothing we can do to help him."

She struck me in the chest and begged us to help him, pleading with us to do something. But there was nothing to be done. No training, no equipment, and no words could change the outcome. That call stayed with me long after the report was written and the shift ended. It changed how I respond to people, how I listen, and how I carry the weight of this profession.

Moments of life and death, regardless of who lives or who dies, define what a real problem truly is. They place everything else into perspective. They reveal how easily people inflate inconveniences into crises and how often discomfort is mistaken for catastrophe. You do not have a real problem if there is a clear and deliberate way to fix it.

A true problem exists when the solution is unclear, uncertain, or impossible. Sometimes the most difficult problems offer no solution at all. The first time you encounter a real problem, it does not feel instructional or enlightening. It feels heavy. It feels final. There is no checklist long enough to guide you through it, and no amount of preparation that makes it manageable. A real problem does not ask for your opinion or your readiness. It simply demands your presence and leaves you responsible for the outcome, even when no outcome feels acceptable. That is when the definition stops being academic and becomes personal.

You learn quickly that tone matters, words matter, and timing matters because you are often standing between someone and the worst day of their life. In those moments, restraint is not weakness. Emotional control is not detachment. They are tools for survival, clarity, and respect for the gravity of what is unfolding in front of you. Those who have lived in proximity to real problems carry themselves differently, not because they believe they are superior, but because their internal scale has changed. They understand the difference between what most people would consider a problem and what a real problem actually is.

This shift in perspective changes how they respond to stress, conflict, and criticism. What appears distant or detached to the outside world is often discipline on the inside. This is one of the reasons the cost of the badge is so often misunderstood. It is not measured only in hours worked, calls answered, or risks taken. It is measured in perspective, a perspective that is permanently altered.

Once you have stood in the presence of a real problem, you cannot unknow it. You carry it into every interaction, every decision, and every moment when others mistake discomfort for disaster.

III

Perspective

The call came in just after midnight: a domestic disturbance with unknown weapons involved. The report from dispatch was brief. Neighbors had heard screaming coming from the house, and then the screaming suddenly stopped. Those words were routine. Too routine. Calls like that blend together after a while, filed away under radio codes and muscle memory. Still, something about the details of the call settled heavily in my chest as my partner and I turned onto the darkened street.

The neighborhood was quiet. Houses sat close together with their porch lights off and curtains drawn. The silence was almost unsettling. We parked a short distance away. As a law enforcement officer, you rarely park directly in front of a house on a call like that. "Distance buys time, and time buys options." A short walk to the front door never hurt anyone. As we approached the house, I could feel my heart rate rising. It was not fear. It was awareness. Perspective sharpens the senses. You begin noticing details that others overlook.

The broken screen on the front window. The slightly open front door. A purse lying in the yard with its contents spilled across the grass. My partner and I slowly pushed the door the rest of the way open, stepped inside the house, and made the standard announcement.

"Sheriff's Office. Make your presence known."

Inside the house, sitting against the kitchen cabinets to the left, was a woman. Her face was swollen, and blood ran from her nose. She looked at us without surprise and without relief. That look hits harder than screaming ever could.

"Where is he?" I asked.

She nodded toward the hallway. Her hands trembled, but her voice remained steady.

"Bedroom."

Every step down that hallway felt deliberate and controlled. This is where perspective overrides adrenaline. Emotions threaten judgment, and discipline steps in to hold the line. The bedroom door was closed, and closed doors always matter. Especially when you are standing in what officers refer to as the "fatal funnel." Many officers have been shot or killed in front of a closed door.

I slowly turned the knob and pushed the door open while cutting the pie, clearing the room from the doorway. Immediately to the left, a man stood near the bed. He was shirtless, sweating heavily, and breathing hard. On the floor beside him sat a black revolver. My mind immediately calculated the situation. If he moved quickly toward the weapon, I would have to kill him. His eyes locked onto mine with a mixture of exhaustion and defiance.

For a split second, the world narrowed to a set of choices. Issue commands and seek concealment, or rush the man and attempt to make an arrest. Homes rarely offer true cover.

Real problems do not give you time to debate philosophy. They demand decisions. I spoke loudly, making every word deliberate.

"Step away from the weapon. Now!"

He hesitated.

That hesitation is where lives are decided. There is a look that people sometimes give when they are prepared to die or when they have simply accepted that the moment has reached its end. As I watched him, several thoughts flashed through my mind. The purse in the front yard. The woman sitting in the kitchen. The knowledge that whatever happened next would follow me home and replay in my head long after the shift ended.

The man let out a sigh and stepped back from the weapon with his hands in the air.

We secured him without further incident. No dramatic takedown. No applause. Just controlled movements and controlled breathing. When it was over, the adrenaline drained from my body all at once, leaving behind the familiar weight that comes after a volatile call. During our search of the house, we found a small child hiding in the back room. She was sitting in the back of a closet, silent, wide-eyed, and alive. She could not have been more than three years old.

Her little face was red from crying, and she looked completely uncertain about the safety of the world around her. It was obvious this was not the first time she had witnessed one of her father's drunken rages. When our eyes met, she immediately lifted her arms toward me the way small children do when they want to be picked up. I felt a wave of sadness for this little girl.

She was not afraid of me. She simply wanted someone to make things feel safe again. I picked her up and placed her on my hip. She wrapped her arms around my neck and began repeating one word over and over.

"Mommy… mommy… mommy…"

All she wanted was her mother. All she wanted was for the night to be over. As I carried her outside, I felt something warm against my left hip. I looked down and realized the child had urinated on herself. She had been so frightened that she could not control it. At that moment, nothing else mattered. My only focus was getting her out of that house and back to her mother.

Outside, neighbors had begun gathering in their yards and on their porches. Some looked relieved. Others looked suspicious. A few stood there recording the scene on their phones, capturing fragments of what had happened without understanding the context behind it. They would talk about what they thought they saw. They always do.

None of them would carry that moment home with them. Later, I sat in my patrol car, sweaty and exhausted, with the left side of my uniform soaked with urine as I drove the child's father to jail. The world does not pause so that you can process perspective. You earn it, and then you keep moving forward.

That night never made the news. No one wrote an article about restraint, judgment, or the decision not to escalate the situation further. The man would face charges. The woman would be offered resources. The child would grow up carrying memories that could never be erased. At the end of my shift, I went home, took a shower, put on clean clothes, and stepped back into normal life as if nothing had happened. This is how perspective is built.

Not through dramatic moments that people imagine from the outside, but through the quiet moments when the wrong decision could have changed everything. Perspective cannot be taught in a classroom. It cannot be issued in general orders or gained through opinion. Perspective is earned.

It is forged in moments where there is no rewind button, no editing, and no second attempt. Once you encounter a real problem, your view of the world changes forever. The inconveniences that once seemed overwhelming become smaller. The frustrations that once provoked anger feel insignificant. You learn quickly that time is not endless, that words matter, and that tomorrow is never guaranteed.

Those who wear the badge live constantly inside the perspective of others. They carry the weight of other people's emergencies long after the call ends, sometimes for the rest of their lives. They attend birthday parties, school events, and family dinners while carrying images in their minds that will never fully fade. This is another cost of the badge, one that never appears in headlines or social media posts. The public often asks why officers sometimes appear guarded, distant, or emotionally reserved. The answer is simple. You cannot repeatedly walk through chaos and expect to remain unchanged.

Despite the scrutiny, law enforcement officers continue to show up for strangers on their worst days. They continue placing themselves between danger and people they may never meet again. Perspective is survival. It is the difference between enduring this profession and being consumed by it. For those who learn to protect it, refine it, and live by it, perspective becomes more than a lesson.

It becomes a legacy.

IV

Knowledge over Arrogance

During the second phase of my law enforcement training as a brand-new deputy sheriff, I learned a lesson that would stay with me throughout my entire career: knowledge is power, and confidence must be built on preparation.

My assigned partner and field training officer was one of the most feared instructors in the agency. He was stern, analytical, deeply knowledgeable in statutory law and case law, physically fit, and a highly respected active member of the SWAT team. He also had a reputation for failing trainees who could not meet his expectations.

To say I was nervous would be an understatement. I was determined not to let him see any sign of vulnerability or uncertainty. My first day unfolded exactly as you might expect. Briefing ended, and we walked out to the patrol car. Before we got in, my training officer turned to me and asked if I had everything I needed. Confidently, I replied,

"Yes, I do."

He paused for a moment and then asked how long I had been in law enforcement. In a slightly arrogant tone, I answered,

"This is my second phase of training. Don't you already know that?"

My response earned the reply it deserved. He looked me straight in the eye and said,

"How the fuck do you have everything you need if you're only in your second phase of training? You don't even know what the fuck you're doing yet, much less have everything you need."

The words hit hard. I was embarrassed. I was angry. What I didn't realize at the time was that this moment would set the tone for the next thirteen shifts, thirteen shifts that would repeatedly humble me, strip away my misplaced confidence, and teach me the difference between believing I was ready and actually being prepared. Next on the agenda was learning my assigned patrol area: Sector 20.

As we drove through the area, my training officer asked how long I had lived there. Without hesitation, I proudly told him that I had lived in the area my entire life and had even worked in a family business located right in that same sector.

He glanced at me and said, "Good. Since you've lived here your whole life and know everything about the area, you don't need this fucking thing." The thing he was referring to was my GPS, mounted to the windshield.

Without another word, he reached over, ripped it off the mount, opened the glove box, tossed it inside, and slammed it shut. The power cord dangled out slightly as the glove box closed.

Then he turned to me and said,

"You will not be using a GPS for the remainder of your time with me, so you better know where you are."

He paused for a moment before continuing,

"If you can't get where you need to go or you get lost, people may die or you might just be lost forever. Either way, you'll figure it out, or I'll fail you out of the field training program."

Almost immediately after he finished speaking, the alert tone sounded over the radio.

Dispatch announced a fight in progress at a trailer village within my patrol zone. I was the only unit available and the call belonged to me.

My FTO looked at me and said,

"Well? What the hell are you waiting for? Let's go."

I'm sure he could see the nervousness on my face.

The truth was terrifyingly simple. I had no idea where that trailer village was, and my GPS was now sitting in the glove box.

After making a great first impression and an even better second one, I activated my lights and siren and started driving toward the call.

I made it about half a mile down the road before taking a right turn.

My FTO immediately shot me an irritated look, reached over, shut off the lights and siren, and said,

"What the fuck are you doing? Pull over."

I sighed as the now familiar feeling of defeat crept in.

Once we stopped, he turned toward me and snapped,

"Where the fuck are you going? Are we going to work today, or are you just going to drive around all day with your head up your ass?"

My frustration and arrogance flared again.

Louder than I should have, I fired back.

"How do you expect me to get somewhere I've never been before with no directions?

He didn't miss the opportunity.

"You told me you've lived here your whole life," he said. "You told me your family business was in this area. Maybe you should've stayed there. I didn't realize you were full of shit and had no idea where you were going."

Then he leaned closer.

"Here's a thought. If you don't know where you're going and you don't have a map, maybe you should stop pretending you know everything and ask for help. Or get out and ask for directions. Or do you think I'm a dumbass who doesn't know where I'm going either?"

For the first time, I felt like I had cracked the code.

I swallowed my pride and took a breath.

"I'm sorry," I said. "Can you please help me? I don't know where I'm going, and we need to get to this call."

He smirked slightly.

"Yeah, I'll help you," he said. "Since you're lost and don't know what the fuck you're doing."

I rolled my eyes behind my sunglasses and stayed quiet.

He stared at me and said, "You gonna go, or are we just gonna sit here until someone kills somebody?"

Eventually, we made it to the call. By the time we arrived, the area was empty. No fight. No people. No one in sight. I radioed dispatch and asked them to attempt contact with the caller again. There was no answer. My FTO looked at me and said, "Congratulations. You took so long getting here that everyone got tired of waiting and left. Hopefully we don't get a call later saying someone was killed."

The remaining ten hours of that shift unfolded exactly as you might imagine. It was going to be a long thirteen days. By my seventh shift with my FTO, things had not improved much. The day had gone terribly, and the previous six shifts had been no better. I was getting lost regularly. I didn't know my patrol zone well enough. My report writing was sloppy and to say I struggled with radio codes and signals was an understatement.

Every mistake felt magnified. I was mentally exhausted and emotionally drained. At one point, I was seriously considering quitting. Most of those feelings were rooted in my own arrogance. I believed I should already be good at the job. I believed I knew more than I actually did. Deep down, however, I knew the truth. If I quit this, I would probably quit everything else in my life whenever things became difficult.

That realization left me trapped in a serious internal conflict. Two hours before the end of that shift, my FTO and I were sitting in the substation conference room with two other FTOs and their trainees. We were all working on reports. Tension was already in the air because of my poor performance that day.

My FTO and I began arguing about my failure to learn my radio codes. I had reached my breaking point. I raised my voice and pushed back harder than I should have. Then my FTO stood up and said something I will never forget.

"How the fuck do you not know these codes?

You're never gonna make it.

Just like you didn't make it at your family's business. Don't worry though I'll have you back there by the end of the week."

Those words crushed me, and I became furious. In that moment, I was ready to punch him in the mouth. The other training officers stepped in immediately, separating us and telling us both to calm down. I had no intention of backing down. Then something hit me with absolute clarity. For the first time in my life, I realized this was a fight I could not win.

Overwhelmed and emotionally drained, I walked out of the room and outside the substation. I got into my car and sat there alone, angry, embarrassed, and unsure whether this moment would define my failure or become the turning point of my life.

After sitting there for a while replaying everything in my head, I looked up and saw my FTO walk out of the building and towards my patrol car.

He pointed at me and said in a stern voice,

"Get out of the car."

I stepped out, ready to quit.

He walked toward me and said,

"Chief, this is it. This is either the turning point, or it's the end. I'm not signing off on your training and putting my name on the soup sandwich you are right now."

Defeated, I told him the truth.

"This is the hardest thing I've ever done in my life," I said.

I admitted that my frustration and arrogance were clouding my thinking and holding me back.

Then he said something I never expected to hear.

"Chief… I'm proud of you."

I was stunned.

He continued.

"I wasn't sure if I was going to have to fail you or if this moment was finally going to happen. I've been trying to break you down so I can build you back up. You're arrogant. You're way too sure of yourself. If I couldn't fix that, you'd never survive in this profession."

Then he said something I will never forget.

"You're ready to work now. Come back on Monday, and we're going to start teaching you how to be a deputy sheriff."

That weekend, I studied harder than I ever had before. I memorized radio codes, learned my patrol zone, and reviewed statutes and case law. For the first time, I wasn't trying to prove myself. I was trying to improve myself.

When I came back to work on Monday, my FTO looked at me, smiled, and said, "Chief, I hope you're ready to learn. Let's go." That day, I learned more in one shift than I had in the previous seven combined. The difference wasn't the material. The difference was my mindset. The walls were down. The arrogance was gone. I was finally open to learning.

Over the rest of my training, I learned interviewing techniques, report writing, investigative skills, and communication strategies that I still rely on today. More importantly, I learned the traits that would define my career: humility, discipline, adaptability, and restraint. Fifteen years later, my FTO and I are still close friends. That Monday morning smile was not approval, it was confirmation. Confirmation that:

I was finally ready to be taught.

Ready to listen.

Ready to survive.

The most impactful mentors are rarely the ones who make you feel good in the moment. They are the ones who see what you could become and refuse to let you remain what you are. My FTO didn't just teach me how to be a deputy sheriff. He taught me how to get out of my own way.

I firmly believe that my FTO's approach may have saved my life long before it was ever in danger, and for that, I am forever thankful.

The power of the mind is extraordinary. One of our greatest tools can also become one of our greatest weaknesses. In law enforcement, you must learn to set feelings aside, think outside the box, and gradually desensitize yourself to things that would otherwise be terrifying. These are not natural human tendencies unless you are a sociopath; your mind and body will resist them at every step. Your body fights night shifts. Your mind rebels against long hours, rotating schedules, twelve-hour shifts, report writing, missed meals, and the constant demand to be proactive while exhausted. This balance, if never learned, can slowly erode an officer from the inside out. Some officers never grasp this reality.

When that happens, the cost can be devastating. It can cost them their sanity. It can cost them their career, and in the worst cases, it can cost them their life. "*When in doubt, don't ever miss the opportunity to shut the fuck up, listen, and remember to always choose knowledge over arrogance.*"

V

Seeing is Believing

Most people, when they hear true law enforcement stories, react with disbelief. Some of the things I have seen would have made me question reality myself if I had not experienced them firsthand. One of the first examples happened in 2014 during my third phase of training in the heart of Sector 20.

My new field training officer and I were dispatched to a disturbance at a local auto parts store, involving a male and a female arguing loudly inside the business. When we arrived, the clerk told us the couple had already left the store and crossed the highway to a nearby street. The clerk pointed toward a young white woman standing near a stop sign and said, "That's her. Not sure where her man went, but that's her." My FTO and I got back into our patrol car and drove across the street to where the woman was standing. As we approached her, it was immediately clear that she had lived a rough life. She was slender with brown hair and light-colored eyes. At one point she might have been considered attractive, but years of methamphetamine use had taken a visible toll on her face, her body, and her behavior. We asked if she was okay.

"Everything's fine," she said. "I don't want your help. I didn't call the cops."

I reassured her that she was not in trouble and that we simply wanted to make sure she was safe. That was when I noticed she kept favoring her right hip near her stomach, occasionally grabbing the area and wincing in pain.

"Is something wrong with your hip?" I asked.

She looked down and said,

"I'm not really sure. I had a really bad sore there, and I think it's infected."

Without warning, she pulled down the top of her pants to expose the area. My FTO and I both nearly lost our composure. There it was a massive open abscess protruding from her skin, surrounded by a dark red and purple ring with a hole that was oozing green and yellow pus. Trying to remain professional, I told her she might want to have EMS take a look at it.

"That looks pretty bad," I said.

Her response caught both of us completely off guard,

"No, I don't need EMS," she said calmly. "I think it's fine now. I got the worm out a few days ago, so it should get better."

I slowly turned toward my FTO, who was seconds away from gagging, and said,

"Chief… are you 10-48 (messaged received) of the worm situation?"

He gagged, laughed, and replied,

"10-4, chief. Worm situation. Got it."

We verified one last time that she did not want medical attention and that she did not wish to report a crime. She declined both. Shaking our heads, we got back into our patrol car. "What in the hell was that?" my FTO asked, half laughing and half horrified. I realized I had to explain botfly larvae to my now traumatized training officer. Ironically, this was one of the few moments where I knew more about something than my FTO, though thankfully not from personal experience, but from books.

I explained that botfly larvae can develop inside the tissue of a living person or animal, creating a large abscess with a small breathing hole in the center. The egg eventually hatches into a tiny white grub-like parasite that feeds on tissue until it matures and exits the body to become a fly. My FTO's face was a mixture of disbelief, disgust, and laughter. I have never forgotten it.

While it is easy to laugh at the absurdity of that moment, the humor was not about mocking her situation. After all, it is not every day that someone hatches a worm and lives to tell the story. To someone outside the profession, law enforcement humor can sound cruel, detached, or inappropriate. Officers may laugh about something shortly after tragedy. They make jokes inside patrol cars after scenes that seem far too serious to laugh about. Humor often grows from misfortune, irony, or the absurdity of human behavior at its worst. From the outside, it looks wrong. From the inside, it is survival.

Law enforcement officers are repeatedly exposed to situations that the human mind was never designed to process in large volumes. Violence, death, cruelty, neglect, and despair are not occasional interruptions in the job; they are routine. They arrive without warning and sometimes leave without resolution. There is no explanation that makes a child's death acceptable. There is no lesson learned that makes domestic violence understandable. There is no way to rationalize a life destroyed in seconds. If every one of those moments were carried with full emotional weight, the burden would eventually become unbearable.

Humor becomes the pressure valve not because the situation itself is funny, but because the alternative is allowing those experiences to hollow you out completely. The humor officers use is rarely directed at victims; more often, it comes from the absurdity of the circumstances or the shared recognition between officers that what they just witnessed makes absolutely no sense. The laughter is not disrespect. It is release.

Real problems rarely end neatly or without consequence. Humor creates enough emotional distance for officers to regain balance and move on to the next call, because another call will always come and another real problem will always demand attention. Humor helps officers transition from one crisis to the next. Misfortune, when filtered through humor, becomes slightly more manageable. It shrinks something overwhelming into something that can be carried and tricks the mind into believing, at least temporarily, that things are still under control. This does not erase empathy; in many ways, it preserves it.

Officers who never laugh do not become more compassionate they become brittle, and brittle things eventually break. There is also an element of trust within this humor. It is rarely shared with the public. Instead, it lives inside patrol cars, briefing rooms, and quiet conversations between officers who understand exactly what it costs to be there. Humor becomes a silent agreement: you're not alone, I saw it too, we're still standing.

This is why attempts to judge law enforcement humor from the outside are often misguided. Without perspective, it sounds like indifference or disrespect. In reality, officers feel deeply, often more deeply than most, but they cannot afford to feel everything all at once. Humor regulates emotion in the same way training regulates action. It prevents emotional overload and preserves clear judgment. Without it, frustration grows, and without release, that frustration hardens into bitterness. Bitterness erodes perspective, and when perspective is lost, mistakes follow.

This profession rarely defeats people through one catastrophic moment. More often, it defeats them through accumulation; call after call, scene after scene, tragedy layered upon tragedy. Humor slows that process. It allows officers to acknowledge pain without surrendering to it. That does not mean every joke is appropriate, nor that humor never crosses a line, but eliminating it altogether would remove one of the few coping mechanisms available in a profession built on absorbing other people's worst moments. Perspective reminds us of this simple truth: *"laughing does not mean we didn't care, it means we cared enough to protect ourselves so we could keep showing up."*

VI

What Goes Up Will Come Down

The saying sounds simple enough: what goes up will come down. Most people use it casually as a reminder that success does not last forever or that momentum eventually fades. In law enforcement, however, that phrase carries a different meaning. It is not philosophical; it is operational, emotional, and learned through experience rather than taught in a classroom. In this profession, things escalate quickly. Adrenaline rises, authority rises, confidence rises and sometimes ego rises with it.

You handle a dangerous call correctly, make a split-second decision that ends without anyone getting hurt, and walk away upright and breathing, knowing you did your job well. In those moments, everything feels sharp and clear. You feel capable. You feel in control. Then gravity reminds you that nothing stays elevated forever. What goes up will come down.

In 2016, I was once again working in Sector 20, this time on night shift, where the real magic tends to happen. Some officers love night shift and stay there for their entire careers.

Others run back to days as quickly as they can. I was indifferent, trouble seemed to know where I was, no matter what shift I worked. It had been a relatively quiet night until about two o'clock in the morning when dispatch sent us to a disturbance call. A neighbor reported a man climbing onto the roof of a church across the street from her house. According to the caller, the man had somehow slid down the metal roof and landed on the church's front awning, where he was yelling, dancing, and jumping while screaming at the top of his lungs.

When we arrived, we saw exactly what the caller described, a barefoot man in his early thirties, wearing a dark T-shirt and jeans, shouting nonsense and bouncing around like he was performing on stage. I looked at my partner and said,

"Chief, this is a situation. What do you think we should do?"

"We should probably call our supervisor," he replied.

His response seemed reasonable. While we waited, we tried to talk the man down. Another officer checked the building and came back shaking his head stating,

"I have no idea how he got up there," he said.

"There are no ladders, no trees, nothing."

I remember thinking, "*well, he didn't get sprinkled with pixie dust and fly up there.*" The more likely explanation was methamphetamine. For the sake of the story, we'll go with the second. When our supervisor arrived and verbal commands failed, she called the fire department for a ladder. When the third responders arrived with the ladder, I asked the obvious question,

"So… who's going up there?"

Without hesitation, she looked at me and said,

"You are and take your little brothers with you."

As a six-foot-four, roughly three-hundred-pound man, I was not thrilled about climbing onto a thirty-five-year-old aluminum awning supported by a few wooden posts, especially with two other deputies. But I wasn't in a position to negotiate.

We climbed up and grabbed the man, moving him to the center of the awning. At that point, there was roughly one thousand pounds of law enforcement standing on a structure that was clearly rethinking its life choices. The man began kicking, punching, and screaming while trying to escape. He launched himself toward the edge, I grabbed his shirt and pants trying to stop him. His weight and momentum nearly pulled me over with him. My utility belt caught on the lip of the awning, leaving us in what I can only describe as a "*full blown situator.*" The suspect was now dangling over the edge, with me hanging onto him, and my partners holding onto me. Eventually, additional officers helped pull him down, and we got him safely to the ground and placed in handcuffs.

Back on solid ground, I looked at the awning. It was bent, warped, and permanently altered. What most people never see is what happens after a high stress call. Once the chaos ends and the reports begin, the mind starts replaying everything. Did I miss something? Did I make the right decision? Did we get lucky? The adrenaline fades, leaving behind exhaustion and reflection.

What goes up must come down and that cycle repeats shift after shift. High risk calls are followed by quiet stretches. Moments where the margin for error is razor thin are followed by hours where nothing happens. The human nervous system was never designed to operate that way. Promotions, praise, and recognition follow the same pattern. They feel good, but they can be dangerous if misunderstood. Ego rises faster than skill if left unchecked, and that kind of thinking gets people hurt.

Law enforcement has a way of humbling people sometimes gently, sometimes not. Officers who believe the climb is permanent tend to fall the hardest. The same principle applies to emotion. Anger rises quickly during volatile encounters. Compassion rises when people are suffering. Neither can remain elevated forever without consequence. Too high leads to recklessness. Too low leads to numbness. Some officers begin chasing the highs: adrenaline, confrontation, control, and confuse intensity with purpose. Eventually, the descent comes: burnout, complaints, bad decisions, and broken relationships.

The lesson is not meant to instill fear but discipline. You learn to anticipate the emotional descent that follows every adrenaline spike. You learn not to make life-altering decisions at emotional peaks. Even on the worst calls, there is an ascent the moment you take control, the moment chaos slows, the moment people look to you for direction. Then the call ends, and you come back down. You sit in the patrol car, breathe, and move on.

Public perception follows the same rule. One day you are the hero; the next day you are the villain. Praise rises, scrutiny follows, and support comes and goes. None of that should dictate how the job is done. If you ride public opinion upward, you will fall with it every time. If you anchor yourself in values, the fall matters less.

The badge does not exempt anyone from gravity. Every rise carries responsibility. Every fall carries a lesson. Those who endure in this profession learn to live somewhere in between allowing confidence without arrogance, emotion without losing control, and success without believing it will last forever. In a profession built on chaos, balance becomes survival. What goes up will always come down.

VII

You Knew

There are moments on certain calls when nothing appears wrong, yet everything feels wrong. No visible threat, no raised voices, and no obvious indicators that something dangerous is about to happen. Just a subtle tension that settles in your chest and refuses to leave. Officers learn quickly that this moment matters. It is quiet. It does not announce itself and sometimes, against better judgment, it is easy to ignore. That feeling is instinct.

Every officer remembers the first time they ignored it. After the situation ends and the adrenaline fades, the thought always creeps back in: You knew something was wrong… and you ignored it. Sometimes ignoring instinct costs safety. Sometimes it costs trust. Sometimes it costs far more.

One example that always comes to mind is a dash camera and body camera video of a fallen officer. The officer had conducted a traffic stop on a suspect with felony warrants who was known to be armed and dangerous. No backup had been requested or dispatched. About one minute into the stop, you could hear it in the officer's voice. Something felt wrong. The officer sensed danger but could not clearly identify what it was. The officer continued with the stop anyway. Within three minutes, the suspect shot and executed that officer on the side of the road. May that officer rest in peace, and may God watch over their family.

Instinct often speaks quietly. It tells you to pause before stepping through a doorway. It tells you to reposition yourself during a conversation. It tells you something about the situation does not feel right. This is not guesswork. This is accumulated experience. Thousands of contacts. Hundreds of tense situations. Dozens of encounters where one wrong move could have ended differently. Instinct is the brain cataloging danger, deception, desperation, and intent.

You feel it when a suspect's compliance appears rehearsed instead of genuine. You notice when eye contact is held too long or avoided entirely. You notice hands drifting toward certain areas of the body for no obvious reason. None of these things alone means much. Together, they create a picture that no training manual can fully explain.

Trust grows through consistency. It grows when officers show up prepared, handle pressure without panic, and do the right thing when no one is watching. There is also danger in ignoring instinct simply to appear confident. Pride has ended more careers than hesitation ever has. Instinct often whispers while ego shouts. Learning which voice to follow becomes part of surviving the job.

Trusting instinct does not mean abandoning procedure. It means applying procedure with awareness. Policies provide a framework, but they cannot predict every moment. Instinct also shapes trust between officers. You quickly learn which partners notice the same details you do and which ones operate on the edge of carelessness. The best partners rarely need long explanations on scene. A glance, a pause, or a shift in position is often enough. Instinct operates silently between them.

Instinct can also protect officers from themselves. It tells you when anger is rising too quickly, when frustration begins clouding judgment, and when the desire to win a confrontation begins replacing the responsibility to resolve it. Recognizing those moments requires humility. It requires restraint. Some officers dismiss instinct as unreliable. They rely strictly on checklists, metrics, and surface-level indicators. *"That works right until it doesn't."* Real problems rarely arrive fully labeled. They reveal themselves slowly.

One incident early in my career taught me that lesson the hard way. At the time, I was assigned to a high-liability unit focused on proactive policing and arrests. I was conducting traffic enforcement when I noticed a driver operating his vehicle without wearing a seatbelt. His windows were down, making it easy to see.

Before activating my emergency lights, I ran the vehicle's tag through the system. The return came back quickly: suspended license. Felony traffic offender. That information alone should have set the tone for everything that followed. Instead, I told myself it was just another routine stop.

I activated my emergency lights. The vehicle slowed down but did not stop. The driver continued creeping forward at two or three miles per hour down a quiet residential street. Slow enough to acknowledge me. Slow enough to delay making a decision. I could see him clearly in the driver's side mirror. He knew I was behind him.

That was the first moment instinct spoke, "you knew". Why isn't he stopping? What is he deciding right now? Is he buying time? Is he planning to run? Fight? Reach for something? The thought passed quickly. Eventually he pulled into a driveway and turned off the vehicle. I should have slowed everything down at that moment. Instead, I stepped out of my patrol car and approached.

The driver was an adult male, around six-foot-four and roughly two hundred pounds. He appeared calm but carried himself with a defensive posture. I explained the reason for the stop: no seatbelt and driving with a suspended license. He immediately denied both. He claimed his license was valid and insisted he had been wearing a seatbelt. Neither statement was true.

That was the second moment, "you knew". People who confidently deny something that can be disproven within seconds are not confused. They are testing boundaries.

The conversation went nowhere. Eventually he accused me of stopping him because of the color of his skin. I did not engage with that accusation. I asked him to step out of the vehicle and place the keys on the roof. He complied. As he stepped out, he grabbed a white grocery bag from the driver's seat containing food items. Nothing illegal. Nothing dangerous. Still, it added another variable to an already unstable situation.

I informed him that he was under arrest for the felony traffic offense and instructed him to turn around and place his hands behind his back. Instead of resisting immediately, the man began crying. He begged me not to take him to jail. Trying to de-escalate the situation, I told him I was sorry but we were still going to jail. Then he made a request,

"Can I take my groceries inside first? My mother lives here, and she won't have food if you take me to jail."

Trying to be reasonable, I told him I would give the groceries to his mother before we left for the jail. He responded by telling me she was not home.

"I'd have to open the door and put them in the refrigerator", he said.

I radioed for backup. Trying to be helpful and ignoring the quiet voice in my head, I agreed to his request. We walked toward the front door together. As we walked, I remember thinking, Great job. You turned a bad situation into a good one. That was the third moment, "you knew".

When he inserted the key into the door and began unlocking it, another thought flashed through my mind. What if he runs inside and locks the door behind him? But by then it was too late. We walked inside the house. The home was neat and well kept. In the living room sat a glass coffee table filled with decorative marbles. A large wooden grandfather clock stood against the wall, and a dark leather couch sat across the room. I followed him into the kitchen.

As he opened the refrigerator and began placing the groceries inside, I noticed a wooden knife block sitting directly beside him on the counter. The thought hit me instantly. If he grabs one of those knives and tries to stab you, you are going to have to kill him. Also, it will be entirely your fault for allowing this situation to happen. Fortunately, he did not grab a knife. He finished putting the groceries away and walked past me toward the front door while calling his mother on his cell phone.

"Mama," he said, crying, "they taking me to jail again. They caught me driving."

When he reached the front door, he shut it and turned toward me. I told him firmly,

"Nope. We're not doing that. Turn around and put your hands behind your back."

He ignored me. When I attempted to grab his wrist to handcuff him, he spun around and punched me directly in the face while still talking on the phone with his mother. I then hit him with a left hook followed by a right hook, stooped down, and grabbed the man around his waist. I then attempted to throw the man to the ground over my right shoulder.

The man's phone went flying, and he was now airborne. While airborne, he kicked one of his legs out, knocking over the large wooden grandfather clock, which had glass in the front of it. The grandfather clock landed on the floor, breaking the glass and some of the wood on the front. When the clock hit the floor, it made a very loud bell-ringing sound. The fight was on.

My intentions of picking the man up and throwing him on the ground behind me over my right shoulder were to land on the floor behind us, but for some reason my trajectory shifted, and we were heading for the glass coffee table full of marbles…There's some good news…

The man landed with his back on the glass coffee table, shattering the fragile legs and the top of the table, sending blue and white marbles everywhere. Needless to say, this was not going well. I landed on top of the man, and we started an all-out brawl on top of the glass from the clock, the wood, the glass from the coffee table, and the marbles. I was able to eventually gain control of the man, flip him over, and place him in handcuffs.

Turns out we both had cuts on our legs, back, hands, knees, and one of us was bleeding under our eye and from our nose. With his blood on me and mine on him, I stood up and told him to stay on the ground. Out of breath and moderately annoyed, here comes the voice in my head again, "Way to go, dumbass, what a great idea this was, you knew this was a bad idea, and you decided to do it anyway. Good luck explaining this one."

Disappointed, I shook my head as my backup, whom I had radioed for earlier, arrived and took the man out of the home and into the back of a patrol car. This whole scenario seemed like it may have been an hour long, but it was only a few minutes. I know you thought the story was over, but I got some more great news for you. I learned from one of my partners that the man requested to go to the hospital due to being cut and bleeding. The man also mentioned he had not one, but two blood-borne diseases. One is the most feared by law enforcement, and the other was a close second. The good news just keeps on coming…

Now I have to go to the hospital to have numerous tests done, and receive the forbidden cocktail otherwise known as Antiretroviral Therapy (ART). This treatment consists of three pills taken once a day for a month that are supposed to help prevent the spread of HIV and some forms of hepatitis. I had heard stories about this medicine and heard that it makes you deathly ill. Obviously, I did not want to be infected by any type of blood-borne pathogen, so I took the medicine. Prior to taking it, I asked the Doctor who was administering it,

"How bad is it?"

To which he replied,

"It's like chemo, but your hair doesn't fall out." More good news……

This profession teaches many lessons the hard way. Trusting instinct is one of the few lessons that offers warning before consequence. When something feels off, it usually is. Listening to that feeling is not a weakness. It is respect for the experience that put it there. Instinct is survival; like perspective, once earned, it must be protected

Obviously, I survived and remain in good health, with no lasting issues. I hope anyone who reads this can learn from my mistake. That traffic stop could very easily have been fatal for any number of reasons, all because I chose to ignore my instincts, suppress the feeling that I shouldn't proceed, and move forward anyway instead of trusting my gut. *"In the end, it really comes down to this: don't be a dumbass, "you knew" better."*

VIII

Train like it Matters

Every officer remembers the moment they first realized that training is not just another requirement of the job it is survival. For some, that realization comes during a foot chase when the body starts moving before the brain fully understands what is happening. For others, it happens on the range when they fumble a reload under pressure and suddenly recognize how easily things could go wrong on the street. The truth reveals itself quickly in this profession: when things go bad, you won't rise to the occasion you will fall back on your training.

That reality alone should be enough to convince every officer to practice the skills this job demands. Such as patrol tactics, shooting, reloading, defensive tactics, less-lethal options, and everything in between. Training is not about looking good on the range or checking a box for the department. It is about survival, consistency, and control when chaos takes over. Too many officers believe experience alone will carry them through difficult situations. Experience does matter, but experience without continued training eventually breeds complacency, and complacency kills.

The street does not warn you about what kind of call is coming next. Dispatch will not tell you that a traffic stop will turn physical, that a disturbance will escalate into violence, or that the next call will test every skill you thought you had mastered. Training is how you prepare for that uncertainty and gives you a chance to stay alive.

Command presence is the foundation of effective law enforcement, yet it is often misunderstood. It is not about volume, intimidation, or ego. Command presence is confidence under pressure. The moment an officer steps out of a patrol vehicle, people begin forming judgments. They assess posture, movement, tone of voice, and eye contact. Within seconds, they decide whether the officer standing in front of them appears capable and in control or unsure and overwhelmed.

If an officer appears hesitant, distracted, or uncertain, that hesitation spreads quickly. Crowds pick up on it, and suspects exploit it. Calm decisiveness, however, often stabilizes a chaotic scene before it has the chance to escalate. Command presence begins the moment you arrive, and it sets the tone for everything that follows.

Establishing control early is critical to both safety and effectiveness. Clear, concise directions reduce confusion and limit opportunities for resistance. Identifying key individuals, separating involved parties, and controlling positioning helps transform disorder into structure. When people understand who is in charge and what is expected of them, compliance increases and volatility decreases. Control does not require unnecessary force; it requires clarity and consistency.

Equally important is controlling the emotional climate around you. Crowds, bystanders, and even fellow officers feed off tension. An officer who remains calm and professional communicates stability. Tone of voice, body language, and eye contact all influence how people respond. When command presence is paired with fairness and respect, it builds credibility, and credibility strengthens authority. In high-risk situations, that credibility can prevent violence before it begins. Command presence is not a personality trait; it is a skill, and like every other skill in this profession, it must be trained.

Firearms training is not just about accuracy; it is about decision-making under stress. It is about drawing your weapon smoothly while your heart rate is racing and adrenaline is flooding your system. It is about reloading without thinking and clearing malfunctions while your hands are shaking. It is also about knowing when not to fire just as much as knowing when you must.

Under extreme stress, the brain does not function the way people imagine it will. Fine motor skills deteriorate, vision narrows, and memory fragments. In those moments, the body defaults to whatever it has practiced most. If you have practiced the right habits, they show up automatically. If you have not practiced them, nothing else will save you.

Reloading, in particular, is often overlooked during training. Yet when rounds run dry at the worst possible moment, fumbling with a magazine is not a minor inconvenience it is a liability. Smooth reloads come only through repetition. Confidence alone cannot replace muscle memory.

Most departments provide ammunition and targets so officers can train outside of mandatory qualification days. Yet many officers rarely take advantage of those opportunities. They are too tired, they do not want to get hot and sweaty, or they do not feel like picking up brass. Range masters across the country often say the same thing: the same handful of officers show up regularly, while many others barely appear until qualification day arrives. Training should not work that way.

A current topic in law enforcement is the increasing use of reflex sights, commonly called mini red dots. Studies show they can improve qualification scores, but a red dot is still just a tool it is not a bullet-guidance system. If an officer struggled with fundamentals before mounting a reflex sight on their firearm, the sight will not magically fix those problems. Fundamentals still matter. Grip matters. Trigger control matters. Equipment should enhance skill, not replace it.

Most modern reflex sights are reliable, but they can still fail. Batteries die, electronics malfunction, and lenses crack. The worst possible time to discover that your equipment is not functioning properly is in the middle of a gunfight. That moment is not a teaching opportunity. Plan for equipment to fail, because when your heart rate is through the roof and the stakes are life or death, excuses will not matter.

Another area of training that is frequently neglected is defensive tactics. It is one of the few skills in law enforcement that you truly cannot train too much. No two fights unfold the same way, and no physical confrontation plays out exactly the way you imagine it will. Train with the goal of staying alive.

If you believe a suspect will never try to take you to the ground, take your firearm, or use it against you, you are mistaken. Consider investing in a martial art outside of department training. In my experience, the most useful and realistic disciplines for officers are judo and Brazilian jiu-jitsu. These sports teach balance, leverage, and control while developing the ability to think and problem-solve under pressure. Those skills matter when situations go sideways and there are no timeouts. Hope is not a strategy, and assumptions get officers hurt.

Less-lethal tools deserve the same respect as firearms. Taser/CEW training is not a backup plan; when used correctly, it can be a life-saving option that prevents serious injury for both officers and suspects. Effective use requires training. Understanding probe spread, distance, deployment angles, and post-deployment control is essential. Poor CEW use can escalate a situation instead of resolving it.

Even simple tools require practice. Flashlight techniques, for example, often seem minor until an officer finds themselves searching a building or clearing a yard in total darkness. A flashlight is not just a tool for seeing; it is a tool for control, identification, and officer safety. Poor lighting decisions can get you ambushed, while good ones can prevent a shooting entirely.

The worst time to discover that your flashlight battery is dead is while chasing someone through the woods at midnight. Check your flashlight at the beginning of every shift, even if you work days. Surprisingly, many day-shift officers do not carry a flashlight at all. Others keep one buried somewhere in the trunk or underneath a seat next to year-old fast-food wrappers. That mindset creates unnecessary risk.

K9 operations are another area frequently misunderstood by officers who do not work closely with canine teams. K9 training is not just for the handler. Every officer working patrol should attend K9 training periodically or practice alongside the K9 team assigned to their shift.

A police dog is not simply another tool; it is a living partner with instincts, limits, and specific handling requirements. Understanding how to operate around a K9 is critical for officer safety, suspect safety, and the safety of the dog itself. Officers must understand where to stand, when to move, and when to give the dog space during deployments. Poor positioning can disrupt a track, interfere with the handler's control, or result in an unintentional bite.

Whenever I worked with a K9 team, I always asked a simple question before beginning a track: "What do I need to know about your dog?" The answer was never exactly the same, because every handler works differently and every dog behaves differently.

I remember one track that reinforced how important that coordination can be. A suspect had fled on foot after abandoning a vehicle during a traffic stop late one evening. A

K9 team was called to assist, and several of us formed up behind the handler as the dog picked up the scent. The dog moved with purpose, pulling steadily along the edge of a wooded area behind several houses. For several minutes the track remained quiet except for the sound of the dog moving through brush.

Suddenly the dog's behavior changed. The handler immediately recognized the shift and signaled for everyone to slow down. Within seconds the dog lunged toward a pile of debris near a fence line where the suspect had been hiding. The suspect surrendered almost immediately once the dog located him. What stood out to me afterward was how smoothly everything unfolded not because it was simple, but because everyone involved understood their role and trusted the dog and handler to do their job. That kind of outcome only happens when officers train together and understand how K9 operations actually work.

K9 tracking requires coordination and trust. The handler reads the dog, the dog reads the environment, and supporting officers must read both. Training together ensures everyone speaks the same language when seconds matter. Understanding canine behavior can also prevent unnecessary force. A well-trained K9 team supported by informed officers can resolve dangerous situations without a single shot being fired. That outcome does not happen by accident it happens because people trained together long before the moment mattered.

Another very real fear for K9 officers is a dog actively apprehending a suspect when a well-meaning officer runs in and deploys a CEW. If a K9 is doing exactly what it was trained to do, biting a suspect, and suddenly receives 50,000 volts to the mouth, the odds of that dog ever apprehending another suspect drop significantly. In that moment, you haven't just shocked a dog. You may have ended a career. This situation could result in the handler losing a K9 partner with whom they have spent over 800 hours in formal training, along with hundreds of additional hours in ongoing weekly training. It may also cost the agency thousands of dollars invested in the selection, purchase, and training of the K9.

Lastly and most importantly, if you are actively tracking with a K9 team and the suspect begins shooting at you, you must move deliberately to the outside of the team and place rounds down range with purpose. Your job in that moment is no longer just staying alive; it's doing so without shooting the K9 handler in the back or the dog that's actively doing its job.

This is not the time for panic, tunnel vision, or wild heroics. You are now responsible for multiple lives moving in close proximity, under stress, while rounds are coming your way.

Precision matters. Awareness matters. I don't say this to scare anyone working a K9 track. I say it because you never want to be the officer remembered for killing their partner and leaving them to die alongside the K9 who trusted them to come home.

Another essential area of training that many officers overlook is grammar and report writing. Report writing may not feel as exciting as firearms training or defensive tactics, but it is just as important. Reports are not just paperwork; they are permanent records.

Months or years after an incident occurs, supervisors, prosecutors, defense attorneys, judges, juries, and investigators may rely on those reports to understand what happened. A poorly written report can undermine an otherwise solid case. Small errors create opportunities for doubt. Vague descriptions, inconsistent timelines, or careless wording can be exploited in court. Defense attorneys look for those weaknesses not because they change what happened, but because they change how the incident is perceived. Clear and detailed report writing protects officers. You never want to be known as the officer who contradicted themself in a report, gave inaccurate information due to job competency, or ended up testifying on behalf of the defense instead of the state.

In critical incidents, reports often become the primary reference long after memories fade. Stress, time, and trauma affect recall, but a well-written report preserves the facts as they were understood at the time. Ultimately, reports shape outcomes. They influence charging decisions, court rulings, administrative reviews, and public trust. Writing clearly and accurately is not just good practice; it is a professional responsibility.

Proficiency in the proper application of a tourniquet is a vital skill that can be lifesaving in emergency situations. Uncontrolled bleeding can result in loss of motor skills, loss of consciousness, and loss of life. You should always become familiar with the specific tourniquet you carry, whether it is a commercially manufactured tourniquet or an improvised alternative. This familiarity ensures correct application under high-stress conditions. Regular practice with placement, tightening, and securing the device promotes muscle memory and enhances confidence, supporting timely and decisive action when needed. As part of personal preparedness, I have always pre-adjusted my tourniquet to accommodate my largest limb and staging it back on my duty belt.

Equally as important is carrying the appropriate medical equipment and having the knowledge to use it effectively. Items such as pressure bandages, hemostatic agents, and gloves are only valuable if you understand their purpose and proper application. Taking the time to learn and periodically review these skills can enhance both your personal safety and your ability to assist others.

Training is not about ego. It is not about proving who is the best shot or the toughest officer on the shift. Training is about preparing for the moment when everything goes wrong and your body reacts before your mind can catch up.

It is about protecting your partners, protecting the public, and sometimes protecting yourself from the worst day of your career. The street does not care how long you have worn the badge. It does not care how many calls you have handled. It does not care about excuses. It only cares about what you can do right now. Training keeps you sharp. Training keeps you humble. Training keeps you alive.

"You do not train because you expect something bad to happen, you train because one day it might. When that day comes, training is the only thing you will have left."

IX

The School Skipper

In 2015, my FTO and I responded to a call from a local high school. The report sounded straightforward enough: two students were skipping class, and one of them, a Hispanic female, was believed to be at her boyfriend's house. On the surface, it seemed like just another truancy call, but that day would become a reminder that appearances in law enforcement are often deceptive.

We arrived at the home just after 10:00 a.m. The driveway was empty, and the house looked deserted. We knocked on the front door, but no one answered. We walked the perimeter to make sure no one was outside in the backyard, then returned to the front door and knocked again. This time, a small Hispanic boy answered. He looked to be around seven or eight years old and was wearing a blue striped shirt and khaki shorts. He had dark hair, dark skin, and curious eyes. Nothing about him seemed alarming.

Through the open door, we could see into a bedroom. A high-school-aged Hispanic male was sitting on his bed, looking at his phone. He was wearing a white T-shirt and black shorts. We asked him to come speak with us, and he calmly replied,

"Y'all can come inside if you want."

The house was small, probably around 1,000 square feet, with a modest living room just inside the front door. A white couch, a coffee table, a television, and scattered toy trucks on the floor made it obvious that children lived there. The home appeared to have two bedrooms and one bathroom. One bedroom door was closed, and the bathroom door was open with the lights off.

As we moved toward the older boy's room, we could smell burnt cannabis, though nothing was visible in plain sight. The boy looked well kept. He had dark skin, neatly groomed short black hair, and a thin mustache. When we asked why he was not at school, he said,

"I didn't feel like going, and we didn't have anyone to watch my little brother, so I stayed home."

I remember thinking that, while kids should not skip school, I at least understood the situation. Someone had to stay with the younger sibling while the parents worked. The older boy seemed nervous, but not in a way that initially felt unusual. He was on edge, but nothing about it seemed extreme. Then we asked the obvious question: was his girlfriend there? His eyes immediately darted toward the kitchen. He hesitated, then said,

"No, she ain't here. It's just my brother."

I pressed further and asked when he last saw her. He hesitated again,

"No," he said.

"There's no one else here."

I clarified the question.

"I'm not asking if anyone is here right now. I'm asking when you last saw your girlfriend."

At that point, he visibly tensed and began rambling about unrelated things. My instinct immediately told me she was there and that he was hiding her. His eyes kept moving everywhere except toward us. More than once, he glanced toward the kitchen. We asked him to come sit in the living room with his younger brother while we contacted their parents. Even after he sat on the couch, he continued looking nervously toward the kitchen.

The kitchen was small and open, with a counter along the inside wall, a stove, microwave, and refrigerator. I also noticed a closet opening with no door. Inside the open kitchen closet was a white cylindrical water heater. We contacted the boys' parents, who advised that they knew the children were home alone but had no other option because they both had to work and had no one to watch the younger child.

After speaking with the parents, the older boy asked if he could go back to his room and get his cell phone from the bed. I told him I would get it for him while he stayed seated on the couch with his brother. I walked into the bedroom, picked up the black cell phone, and began walking back toward the living room. As I passed through the kitchen, I noticed something beside the water heater in the open closet. At first, I could not tell exactly what I was seeing. It was dark in color and appeared to be wedged between the wall and the water heater. It looked out of place.

I walked back to my partner and quietly told him what I had seen. He told me to stay with the boys, and he went into the kitchen and shined his flashlight into the closet.

A moment later, I heard him yell,

"Come out of there! Let me see your hands!"

I turned so I could keep both boys in sight on the couch while also watching the kitchen. A light-skinned white female with orange-red hair and freckles emerged from behind the water heater. She was wearing a black hooded sweatshirt, dark blue jeans, and purple socks with no shoes.

When asked who she was, the older boy muttered,

"Just a friend... she's scared we were going to get caught and go to jail."

I remember thinking, Jail? For skipping school? Really? Juveniles can be arrested for truancy, but that typically comes only after numerous missed days and multiple warnings to both the parents and the child. That was not the situation here. At the time, I assumed the boy was simply misinformed and overreacting. The girl came over with my partner and sat on the couch with the two boys. She was visibly shaking and appeared incredibly nervous given the circumstances. We ran all three names through the system. None of them came back with warrants or probation violations.

We then notified the boys' mother that we had found another person hiding in the home and advised her she needed to come home from work. The white female called a family member, who came and picked her up. A short time later, the boys' mother also returned to the house.

I completed a report documenting the truancy, the young children being left home alone, and the girl hiding behind the water heater. My partner and I talked about the call off and on throughout the rest of the day, still puzzled by how nervous both the older boy and the girl had seemed. At the time, we chalked it up to fear and teenage overreaction.

Three weeks later, I came across a news article that made my stomach drop. The article included photographs of the older Hispanic male and the white female we had encountered that day. The headline read:

Teens Arrested for Murder.

It turned out that just days before our visit the boy and girl, along with another friend, had lured an adult man into a car and drove him to a remote orange grove near a phosphate pit. The older boy we had met in person was involved, as was the girl we found hiding behind the water heater.

Neither the article nor the arrest affidavits initially spelled out every detail, but it was later determined that the older Hispanic male we had contacted at his home switched places with his friend and began driving. The white female later stated that she got out of the vehicle on the side of the road to urinate. According to her statement, the older boy, his friend, and the victim drove farther down the dirt road. While she was urinating, she heard a gunshot. She said the two returned to pick her up afterward.

She later testified that one of the Hispanic males had executed the older man in the passenger seat. She also stated that one of the suspects later drove the victim's vehicle into a phosphate pit, submerging it. After her arrest, she admitted that she later sold the murder weapon, a .38 handgun, to a local drug dealer.

Looking back, that call taught me an unforgettable lesson: nothing is ever as simple as it first appears. The nervous glances, the hesitation, the tension in the room all of it meant something far darker than a truancy call could have suggested. If something feels off, it probably is.

There was no way we could have known what had happened in the days before we arrived. On the surface, it was ordinary: a couple of kids skipping school. Nothing about the neighborhood, the family, or the house screamed danger. Yet in law enforcement, ordinary calls often conceal hidden depths, and quiet scenes can be some of the most dangerous of all.

Inside, everything seemed normal at first glance. A small living room, scattered toys, a teenager on his phone, a younger sibling watching quietly. The smell, the clutter, and the nervous energy all appeared typical of a household with children left home alone. But instinct was already whispering that something else was there. The hesitation in his answers, the repeated glances toward the kitchen, the subtle avoidance in his voice those were breadcrumbs. At the time, we did not yet understand where they led.

We had no way of knowing that behind a water heater, a girl was hiding for reasons we could not begin to imagine. We had no way of knowing that this simple truancy call touched the edge of something much darker. The danger was real. It was simply hidden, waiting in silence.

Had the older boy or the girl believed we were there to arrest them for murder, the situation could have changed instantly. They could have started shooting. They could have taken the younger child hostage. One misread move, one incorrect assumption, and the entire call could have become a disaster before we even understood what we were standing in.

That day reinforced a truth every officer eventually learns: in law enforcement, appearances are rarely the full story. Ordinary calls can conceal extraordinary danger. The unknown often sits quietly just out of sight until the moment it makes itself known. It was a lesson in vigilance, humility, and respect for the unseen and the unanticipated.

X

Car or Coffin

In law enforcement, a patrol vehicle is far more than transportation. It is cover, concealment, communication, and, at times, the only thing standing between you and serious harm. Too often, officers think of the patrol car merely as the thing that gets them to the call rather than as a tactical asset once they arrive. That mindset can get people hurt.

Understanding the difference between concealment and cover is critical. A patrol car can provide both, but not equally and not in every location. Doors, pillars, and engine blocks offer the best chance of stopping rounds. Sheet metal, windows, and trunk lids do not. Knowing where to position yourself in relation to your vehicle can be the difference between actual protection and a false sense of security. Training teaches you where the car can save you and where it cannot.

Positioning your patrol car matters just as much as how you use it. Angling the vehicle during traffic stops, perimeter assignments, or on high-risk calls can provide cover while limiting a suspect's ability to approach or escape. Poor positioning leaves you exposed. Good positioning buys time, distance, and options. Those few seconds matter more than most people realize.

Close-quarters combat around vehicles during traffic stops is one of the most volatile and unforgiving environments an officer can face. A patrol vehicle or a suspect's vehicle is not just transportation. It becomes concealment, limited cover, a weapons platform, and an obstacle all at once. In a sudden gunfight, distance is minimal, reaction time is compressed, and angles are restricted by the geometry of the vehicles themselves. Officers must remain conscious of backdrop, crossfire risks with assisting units, and the suspect's ability to move quickly around the vehicle, reenter it, or retrieve a weapon. Where you park, how you approach, and where you stand often determine survivability if rounds are fired.

Physical confrontations near vehicles present a different but equally dangerous challenge. Tight spaces limit movement. Footing can be compromised by curbs, gravel, or debris. Suspects can use door frames, seat belts, or the interior of the vehicle to anchor themselves and resist arrest. Weapons may be hidden within arm's reach, and a suspect who breaks contact can transition instantly from fighting to fleeing or to accessing a firearm. Officers must maintain awareness of their position relative to the suspect, the vehicle's doors, and passing traffic while avoiding tunnel vision during the struggle. Close-quarter encounters around vehicles demand disciplined tactics, constant situational awareness, and the ability to move seamlessly between verbal control, physical engagement, and lethal force if necessary.

Communication and coordination under stress are equally critical. During a confrontation involving vehicles, officers must clearly articulate movements, positions, and threats to assisting units in order to prevent confusion or crossfire. Simple statements such as "driver's side," "passenger moving," or "gun!" can prevent tragedy. Maintaining visual control of a suspect's hands, managing distance when possible, and resisting the urge to crowd a vehicle without tactical advantage are essential principles. In these compressed encounters, hesitation can be deadly, but so can overcommitment. Training that realistically replicates the chaos of traffic stop engagements is vital to developing the judgment and restraint required to survive them.

Driving under stress is another skill that cannot be improvised. When adrenaline spikes, fine motor skills deteriorate and tunnel vision begins to set in. The ability to control speed, steering, braking, and situational awareness while your heart rate is elevated must be developed through repetition. Without training, stress turns driving into a liability rather than an advantage.

Emergency driving adds another layer of risk. Lights and sirens do not make you invincible. They demand greater responsibility. Intersections, blind curves, and unpredictable civilian drivers create danger zones that have ended careers and lives. Knowing when to push and when to slow down is a judgment call shaped by training and experience, not by impulse.

Pursuit driving deserves special respect. Chasing another vehicle is one of the most dangerous things an officer can do. Motor vehicle incidents remain a leading cause of line-of-duty deaths for law enforcement officers almost every year. Pursuits require discipline, communication, and a clear understanding of policy and risk versus reward. Speed alone does not win pursuits. Coordination does. Knowing when to back off can be just as important as knowing how to stay in the chase.

"You do not have to outspeed the suspect. You only have to outdrive them."

Equally important is knowing your vehicle's limits. Every patrol car handles differently. Weight, braking distance, acceleration, and turning radius all change depending on equipment load, passengers, and road conditions. Rain, sand, gravel, and worn tires can turn a routine maneuver into a crash scene. Training teaches you what your vehicle can and cannot do before the street forces you to learn the hard way. Some patrol cars feel like they are floating off the ground at high speed. Others feel glued to the pavement. You need to know which one you are driving.

Officers must also know their vehicle inside and out. In high-stress moments, you will not have time to search for gear. You should know by feel alone where your rifle is mounted, where your less-lethal tools are stored, where your medical gear is located, and how to access all of it from different positions. Seconds spent fumbling are seconds you may not have.

The same principle applies to the controls inside the car. Emergency lights, siren tones, radio functions, MDT placement, and spotlight operation should all be second nature. Dividing your attention between driving and operating equipment increases risk if those tasks are not practiced until they become automatic. Training builds that familiarity so your attention can remain focused where it belongs outside the vehicle.

Your patrol car is also a mobile command post. It carries information, provides communication, and creates a visual presence that can either stabilize or escalate a scene. How you arrive matters. How you park matters. How you exit matters. Every movement sends a message to suspects, bystanders, and your fellow officers.

Felony takedowns are another area where training cannot be optional. These are high-risk, high-stress encounters where communication, positioning, and coordination save lives. Everyone has a role, and everyone needs to know it before the first command is ever given. When officers hesitate or contradict each other, suspects can recognize it and exploit it. Practice with your shift partners and supervisors. One of the most frustrating things at the end of a pursuit or during a felony stop is hearing three officers yell three different commands at a suspect who is trying to surrender. Pick one voice. Traditionally, that should be the first officer positioned directly behind the stopped vehicle.

Some agencies issue pool cars. Others assign take-home vehicles. Either way, the responsibility is the same. Check your oil. Check your tire pressure.

Everyone knows that officer the one with wrappers, empty bottles, and random nonsense stacked so high in the vehicle they could probably lose a passenger in it. Do not be that person. Your patrol vehicle serves as your workspace for the duration of a twelve-hour shift, making its condition an important reflection of your professional readiness. When the vehicle is cluttered or disorganized, it can contribute to scattered thinking and may even influence personal presentation. Maintaining an orderly environment supports clear, focused decision-making, whereas disorganization has a tendency to carry over into other aspects of performance.

It is also worth mentioning that every time you remove a suspect or passenger from the back seat of your patrol car, you need to thoroughly inspect that area. This is non-negotiable. Taking an extra thirty seconds to check can save you a tremendous amount of trouble. You would be surprised how many officers have found needles, keys, baggies, drugs, and even firearms in the back seat of a patrol car after transporting someone who had supposedly been searched.

At the end of the day, your vehicle is not just a tool. It is part of the fight. It can protect you, betray you, or save you depending on how well you understand it. Training transforms the patrol car from a mode of transportation into a tactical advantage. Know your vehicle. Respect its limits. Use it with purpose. Because when things go bad, it may be the only cover you have and the only reason you make it home.

XI

Is Somebody Watching?

Integrity is the invisible part of the badge. Nobody can see it, but everyone feels it. It is the difference between an officer who earns respect and one who loses trust before the end of a single shift. I have seen both, and the gap between them can be measured in one decision, one action, or one overlooked rule. Early in my career, I heard story after story about officers who were fired, arrested, and stripped of everything because they misplaced evidence, mishandled money, showed up to work intoxicated, or made other reckless decisions they believed would never catch up to them.

Small compromises are the silent killers. Skipping a report, bending a procedure, or "covering" for a buddy starts small. You tell yourself it is just this once. Before long, it becomes a pattern, and suddenly your judgment is questionable in everything you do. I have watched officers go from respected, to reprimanded, to unemployed because they believed one little shortcut would not matter. Spoiler: it always matters.

Off-duty life can be just as dangerous to integrity as anything that happens on shift. I have known officers who posted things online that made the department cringe, joked publicly about active cases, associated with the wrong crowd, or loudly expressed opinions that reflected poorly on the agency. Social media does not forget, people notice, and when the day comes to make a difficult call, everyone remembers who is credible and who is not.

Substance abuse is another trap. I have seen officers rationalize drinking after a hard shift, thinking no one would notice. But impaired judgment does not clock out when you do. One bad decision made under the influence can destroy a career faster than almost anything else. Years of hard work can be undone in a single night.

Self-awareness is not optional. Stress, fatigue, and personal issues cloud judgment. Recognize when your decision-making is compromised and seek help before it affects your integrity. Asking for help is not weakness. It is one of the strongest moves you can make.

Even good intentions can lead you into ethical gray areas. Pressure from a partner, a desperate citizen, or even a supervisor can make the wrong decision sound reasonable. I have been in situations where saying no was much harder than saying yes. Saying no is rarely glamorous, but it is often the right choice.

Infidelity is another personal failure that can quietly destroy an officer's professional integrity. Relationships built on secrecy, lies, or betrayal eventually spill into the workplace. Partners, supervisors, and fellow officers notice when someone is distracted, emotionally compromised, or making irrational choices. I have seen good officers put themselves and their careers at risk because personal failures created stress, divided attention, and poor judgment. Maintaining honesty and accountability in your personal life matters just as much as maintaining it on the job.

I have also learned that inappropriate actions whether physical, emotional, unintentional, or even words spoken as jokes can have lifelong consequences. They can damage your family, your career, and your reputation, leaving stains that may never fully disappear. Learn from my mistakes, and from the countless mistakes made by officers and supervisors before you. Many people, myself included, are not innocent in this. A decision that compromises your integrity can and most likely will change the course of your life.

You may rebuild trust. You may change your behavior. You may repair relationships and move forward from certain choices. But the guilt of decisions made in the moment can linger forever. It becomes a weight you carry every day, one that does not fully disappear.

Do yourself a favor: resist impulses, ignore persuasive voices that seem harmless in the moment, and think carefully before acting. Protect your family, protect your career, and most importantly, protect your conscience. The consequences of poor decisions are often permanent, and some burdens are simply unnecessary. Guard yourself. Make wise choices. Do not give yourself regrets that will follow you for the rest of your life.

So how do you stay on course? Awareness. Be conscious of every decision. Ask yourself a simple question: *Would I defend this action in court, in front of my family, or to the person I respect most in this profession?* If the answer is anything less than a confident yes, do not do it, and yes, that sometimes means swallowing your pride or facing conflict.

Documentation is your friend. Write everything down. Be honest in every report, even when it is inconvenient. Own your mistakes immediately. Pretending something did not happen, minimizing it, or twisting the facts will always catch up to you. It does not matter how minor it seems. The truth is the backbone of credibility. If you did not document it, it never happened.

Mentorship matters too. Find officers who model integrity, study how they carry themselves, and ask questions. I have learned more from watching good officers navigate difficult situations than any classroom ever taught me. Their calm, consistent adherence to standards became the map I followed. Peer accountability matters just as much. If a partner cuts corners, address it professionally and safely. Silence becomes consent, and in law enforcement, consent can have consequences that extend far beyond paperwork.

Training and continuous education matter as well. Knowing the law, understanding procedure, and respecting ethical boundaries help keep you grounded. Confidence built on knowledge reduces the temptation to cut corners. Officers who are unsure of themselves are often the ones most tempted to "figure it out later." That is when problems begin.

Integrity is not a one-time achievement. It is a daily practice. Every call, every interaction, and every report is an opportunity either to reinforce it or to chip away at it. Most days it feels subtle. Some days it feels invisible, but when the moment arrives that truly tests it, your past choices suddenly matter more than any piece of equipment you carry.

Officers who maintain integrity build careers, reputations, and a sense of personal pride that nothing can take from them. Those who compromise it even slightly risk everything: their badge, their family, their livelihood, their freedom, and sometimes even their children's trust in who they are. There are no do-overs when public trust is lost.

Integrity is about how you carry yourself when no one is watching, how you make decisions when the outcome is uncertain, and how you come home after carrying the weight of other people's worst moments. At the end of the day, integrity is the most important tool you carry. You can replace a radio, a gun, or a patrol car. You cannot replace credibility. Guard it. Practice it. Defend it. In law enforcement, the badge is not just metal. It is the trust people place in you every single day. Lose that, and nothing else matters.

XII

Earn Your Edge

No one will ever care more about your career than you do. In law enforcement, waiting for permission, approval, or direction before investing in yourself is one of the fastest ways to fall behind. Agencies do their best to train officers to minimum standards, but minimum standards are not the same as professional excellence. If you want more, you have to advocate for yourself.

Being your own advocate means recognizing gaps in your knowledge and taking responsibility for closing them. It means understanding that your safety, your credibility, and your long-term success depend on more than what you learned in the academy or during field training. Policies change. Tactics evolve. Threats adapt. Officers who stop learning fall behind quickly, often without realizing it.

Agency-approved training matters, but it is limited by staffing, budgets, and liability concerns. Many departments simply cannot provide the depth or variety of education officers need to thrive in specialized or evolving roles. That is not always a failure of leadership. Often, it is just the reality of the profession. The responsibility to grow beyond the minimum still falls on you.

Furthering your education does not always mean earning a college degree or collecting formal certifications, though those can certainly be valuable. Education can be as simple and as powerful as reading the right books, listening to experienced professionals, studying case law, or learning from people outside law enforcement. Knowledge compounds quietly, but its effects show up clearly when decisions have to be made under pressure.

Reading books on tactics sharpens your ability to think instead of just react. But reading alone is not enough. Tactical concepts may be understood through books, but they cannot be properly executed without live training. Use what you learn. Practice it on the range or in a shoot house. Understanding movement, angles, timing, distance, and human behavior gives you options when situations become unpredictable. Officers who have studied multiple approaches are rarely locked into one plan and are less likely to become overwhelmed when the original plan fails.

Books on interviewing and interrogation teach much more than how to ask questions. They teach patience, psychology, discipline, and observation. They show how people communicate under stress and how truth often reveals itself through inconsistencies, silence, or small details. These skills do not just solve cases. They also prevent tunnel vision and protect you from false assumptions. Things are rarely as simple as they first appear. Anyone who has ever worked with me knows that interviewing suspects is one of my favorite things to do. There is something exhilarating about getting someone to tell you something that they do not want to tell you. Especially when they tell you and they do not even realize it.

Education in any field you are passionate about has value. Whether it is K9 operations, firearms, investigations, leadership, defensive tactics, crisis intervention, or officer wellness, depth matters. When you pursue knowledge voluntarily, it becomes personal. When learning becomes personal, it becomes instinctive under stress. Everyone has excuses. The better question is this: why would you not go the extra mile to sharpen your edge?

Being your own advocate also means seeking opportunity instead of waiting for it. Volunteer for extra training. Ask to sit in on interviews. Request ride-alongs with specialized units. Find mentors. Ask questions. You may hear no repeatedly, but persistence demonstrates commitment, and commitment is rarely ignored forever.

One of the biggest mistakes officers make is limiting themselves to what is required. Policy training is necessary, but it often teaches compliance rather than mastery. True professionalism grows from curiosity from the willingness to ask, *what else can I learn?* even when there is no immediate reward. To this day, I still have a stack of training requests that agencies never approved. That stack serves as a reminder that whether a request gets approved or not, you can always continue educating yourself through books, podcasts, peer mentorship, reading reports, and studying statutes and case law.

Some officers avoid extra education because they fear standing out or being labeled overly ambitious. In this profession, that fear is misplaced. Competence earns trust. Preparation builds confidence and confidence grounded in knowledge makes you safer, calmer, and more effective when others are not. Self-education also serves as legal and ethical armor. Officers who understand case law, constitutional limits, and use-of-force principles are far less likely to make preventable, career-ending mistakes. Knowledge does not eliminate risk, but it dramatically reduces the number of errors you could have avoided.

Reading and learning outside your own agency broadens your perspective as well. It exposes you to different leadership styles, tactical philosophies, and operational models. That wider view challenges complacency and helps you adapt. Being your own advocate also requires humility, the understanding that no matter how long you have worn the badge, there is always more to learn. The moment an officer believes they have nothing left to gain is the moment growth stops and risk begins increasing.

Your personal growth will not always align with your department's promotion cycle or the timing of specialized assignments. That does not mean your development should stop. Every book you read, every concept you study, and every skill you refine moves you forward whether anyone else notices it or not. There will be days when fatigue, burnout, or frustration make learning feel like a burden. Ironically, those are often the days when it matters most. Education restores purpose. It reconnects you to the profession beyond shift work, reports, and the constant cycle of calls.

The officers who thrive long term are rarely the most naturally gifted. They are the most prepared. They invest in themselves quietly, consistently, and deliberately. They understand that learning is not a phase. It is a career-long obligation.

Some people reading this may believe law enforcement is the hardest job they have ever had. I certainly felt that way when I first started. But through agency training, self-directed study, reading, real-world experience, and a willingness to keep learning, the job eventually became second nature to me. It is rare now that I find myself without an answer. If I do find myself without the answer, I am willing to find someone smarter than me and learn it. Never let anyone shame you for asking questions and pursuing knowledge.

You owe it to yourself to exceed the minimum. You owe it to your partners to be capable and dependable. Most importantly, you owe it to the public to be informed, disciplined, and professional. Be your own advocate. Read widely. Train intentionally. Learn relentlessly. Do not limit yourself to what is offered or approved. The knowledge you pursue on your own may one day save your reputation, your career, or your life.

XIII

The Barking Chicken

One of the most important and least discussed skills in law enforcement is knowing who to distance yourself from. This profession exposes people under pressure, and pressure reveals character quickly. Not everyone wearing a badge is moving in the same direction, and not everyone who speaks loudly is worth listening to.

In recent years, a growing danger has taken hold inside many agencies: officers who prioritize social media attention over professional competence. These individuals chase likes, followers, and online validation while neglecting the fundamentals of the job. Policing is not a performance, and the street is not a stage. *"When attention becomes the goal, judgment becomes the casualty."*

Officers who pursue social media fame often take unnecessary risks, exaggerate their experiences, or blur ethical boundaries for the sake of a story. They film, post, or speak without considering investigations, victims, or officer safety. Even passive association with that kind of behavior can drag you into scrutiny you never asked for and consequences you did not earn.

Another group to be cautious of is the loud, boisterous officers who speak with total confidence but lack real knowledge. Volume is often mistaken for competence. These people dominate conversations, interrupt training, and dismiss expertise they do not possess. Over time, their certainty becomes contagious and dangerous.

In critical moments, these officers rely on bravado instead of preparation. They oversimplify complex situations and ridicule caution as weakness. When things go wrong, they are often the first to deflect blame. Learning from someone like that does not sharpen you. It dulls you, and in some cases, it can get you killed.

Equally damaging are those who allow ego to stain the badge. Ego-driven officers believe the rules apply differently to them. They see correction as disrespect and accountability as a personal attack. Over time, that entitlement breeds misconduct and poisons teams. It creates resentment, fractures trust, and turns shared missions into personal competitions. Officers driven by ego are rarely interested in growth. They are interested in being perceived as superior.

You also need to distance yourself from officers who are quick to anger and default to violence. Emotional volatility has no place in a profession built on restraint, judgment, and control. An officer who cannot manage their temper will eventually force others to manage the fallout. These individuals often justify their aggression as strength or decisiveness. In reality, it is usually insecurity wearing authority. They escalate situations unnecessarily and put partners at risk physically, legally, and professionally. There are absolutely times when force is necessary, and it is possible to have good intentions that look bad on camera. But when that becomes a pattern, it is no longer a coincidence. It is a warning sign.

Perhaps one of the most dangerous types to avoid is the officer who pretends to be tactically sound. These individuals speak in buzzwords, repeat phrases from training they barely understand, and posture as experts without the experience to support it. They sound convincing until reality tests them. They tend to have the cool gear, fancy guns, and a lot to say about their latest range day. In my experience, however, some of the most tactically dangerous and capable officers are the quiet ones. They do not advertise it. They simply know what they are doing and use the equipment their agency gave them.

Fancy guns, cool gear, the newest morale patch, and loud obnoxious behavior do not win gunfights. More often than not, the people who perform that way are nowhere to be found when the shooting starts.

Most troubling are the officers who claim victories that were never theirs. They tell stories about high-risk incidents they barely participated in or completely fabricate involvement in calls they only heard about later. They wear other people's courage like borrowed medals. That is not harmless storytelling. It is deception.

When officers inflate their experience, they mislead younger officers, supervisors, and even themselves. Worse, they can end up in leadership or instructional roles they have no business holding, where they spread bad habits and misinformation to others. Associating closely with these people puts your own credibility at risk. In law enforcement, reputation is built slowly and destroyed quickly. Guilty by association is real. When someone's stories unravel, everyone tied to them gets questioned.

There is also a broader cultural cost. These personalities often dominate locker rooms and briefing rooms, crowding out thoughtful voices and discouraging humility. Over time, silence replaces accountability and professionalism gives way to performance. Distancing yourself from people like this does not mean isolating yourself or acting superior. It means being intentional about who influences your thinking, your habits, and your reputation. Not every coworker deserves a seat at your mental table.

The officer's worth staying close to are usually quieter. They ask questions. They listen more than they talk. They do not advertise their experience because they do not need to. Their competence shows up when it matters, not when it is convenient. Strong professionals do not rush to anger. They do not chase recognition. They do not exaggerate. They focus on preparation, teamwork, and accountability. Being around people like that naturally raises your standards.

Choosing distance also protects your integrity. When misconduct happens and it eventually will, investigators look at associations, conversations, and culture. Being known as someone who avoids drama matters more than people realize. There will be times when distancing yourself feels uncomfortable. You may be labeled quiet, distant, or "not one of the guys." Accept that. Temporary discomfort is far better than permanent damage.

Law enforcement careers end in many ways. Some end with retirement and pride. Others end in internal affairs files, courtrooms, and lifelong regret. The people you surround yourself with often influence which path you take more than any one decision ever will.

You cannot control who works beside you, but you can control who you emulate, who you trust, and who you follow. Wisdom in this profession often comes down to knowing who not to listen to. Distance yourself from noise. Distance yourself from ego. Distance yourself from anger disguised as confidence and stories disguised as experience. None of those things will protect you when everything goes sideways. Protect your reputation as fiercely as you protect your safety.

"Choose mentors over performers. Choose substance over volume. Choose integrity over attention."

XIV

Down Range

It was early March, just before 5:50 a.m., and I was finishing a report from a call I had handled the previous day. I was parked outside the receiving bay of the local hospital, trying to wrap up paperwork before the natives began their usual tomfoolery and criminal actives. The morning was quiet until the alert tone shattered it. Dispatch sent me to an armed disturbance.

I remember thinking how strange the call sounded. It was a Sunday morning, not even six o'clock yet. What could possibly be happening at that hour? The call was in a townhome community that rarely generated calls for service. It was a quiet area with more than a hundred two-story units, well-kept and usually uneventful.

I activated my lights and siren and started toward the call. While I was en-route, dispatch updated the information. An ex-boyfriend had reportedly broken into a residence and was threatening the caller's mother with a gun. The caller was the victim's adult daughter. According to dispatch, the suspect had entered through the back sliding glass door after smashing it with a tire iron, and he was now holding the victim at gunpoint.

Because I could not hear the caller directly only the dispatcher relaying the information I could not judge her tone for myself. Over the years I had responded to plenty of calls where someone claimed a weapon was involved simply to get officers there faster, only for no weapon to exist at all. That possibility crossed my mind. Even so, based on the seriousness of the information, I continued responding in emergency mode.

While driving, I began a mental scene assessment. I thought about the layout of the community, the time of day, and the likelihood that nearby residents might be outside walking dogs or getting ready for work. I also thought about staffing. We were between shifts. Night shift was either tied up or heading home, and day shift was still coming in. Backup would be limited, at least at first.

I also considered crossfire. If rounds were fired outside, there would be townhomes, parked cars, and potentially uninvolved residents in the background. Before I ever arrived, I made the decision that I would deploy my patrol rifle. If precision shooting became necessary, I wanted the rifle in my hands.

Dispatch continued feeding updates. The situation sounded like it was escalating quickly. The caller now reported that the suspect had a gun pressed to her mother's head and was threatening to kill her. Dispatch also advised that the daughter was pretending to be on the phone with her employer calling out of work so the suspect would not realize she was actually speaking with law enforcement.

When I entered the community, I parked on the northwest side of the complex, about sixty yards away from the incident location. My zone partner arrived moments later and parked behind me. I stepped out and told him I was grabbing my rifle.

I retrieved my AR-15, chambered a round, and confirmed the magazine was seated. I placed an extra magazine in my left rear pocket. I hoped I would not need it, but the time to realize you need more ammunition is not when you are already pinned behind cover. Dispatch then advised that the suspect and the victim were now outside on the intersecting street just to my left.

It was still dark. The streetlights gave us only limited illumination, and dawn was still twenty minutes away. I adjusted the brightness on my red dot to fit the lighting conditions. My partner moved ahead on the west sidewalk, about fifteen steps in front of me, while I walked south down the center of the roadway with parked vehicles between us. We had covered only about fifteen yards when a female suddenly emerged from between two parked cars on the east side of the street. It was the caller's mother.

She was wearing a white short-sleeved T-shirt and white pajama pants with blue and pink feather patterns on them. Her hands were raised around shoulder level, and she looked directly at my partner and calmly said;

"Everything is okay. Everything is fine."

I stopped immediately and assumed a shooting stance. Her sudden appearance, combined with the information we had received, left too many unknowns.

My partner motioned for her to come toward him and asked,

"Ma'am, come over here. Where is he?"

The moment those words left his mouth, she snapped her head over her left shoulder, then turned back and began sprinting toward him. She only made it a few steps before I saw a male emerge from between the same two vehicles behind her. He was chasing after her. He was wearing blue jeans and a white button-up shirt. His right arm was extended, and in his hand, I could clearly see a black handgun pointed in the direction of the woman and my partner.

From the moment the woman stepped out to the moment I saw the suspect was no more than five seconds. I disengaged the safety on my rifle, acquired my sight picture, and placed the red dot on the suspect's upper torso near the shoulder. Almost instantly, I saw a bright muzzle flash and heard a gunshot. The woman collapsed forward, her momentum carrying her onto the pavement. I fired my rifle until the suspect went to the ground. The air filled with smoke and the smell of gunpowder. I immediately radioed,

"Shots fired. Shots fired. Suspect down. I got one hit. Send EMS."

I ran toward my partner and the two bodies in the roadway. The woman lay in front, with the suspect just behind her, nearly touching. My partner emerged from cover between the vehicles, where he had moved after the suspect fired in his direction.

When I reached the suspect, I saw the handgun lying on the ground above him. There was a significant amount of blood on the front of his shirt, his head, and his right arm. I checked for a pulse. There was none. I shined my rifle light into his open left eye. The pupil was fully dilated, and there was no pupillary response.

He was dead.

I then turned to the woman. Bright red blood was pouring from her right hip. I told my partner to roll her slightly and apply pressure while I radioed dispatch again and requested an AED. At that moment, I noticed another person standing within a few feet of us. It was the daughter. She was hysterical, screaming and crying. She had just watched her mother's ex-boyfriend shoot her mother, followed immediately by me killing him.

I will never forget her face.

I will never forget her screams.

Amid the chaos, I heard my lieutenant ask over the radio whether everyone on scene was okay. I replied calmly,

"The suspect is dead."

EMS arrived and transported the woman to the hospital, where she was later pronounced deceased. More officers began arriving, securing the scene, shutting down the roadway, and identifying witnesses. I remained near the suspect until I felt someone pulling on my left arm. Flooded with adrenaline, I instinctively pulled away, still focused on the scene. Then I felt someone grab the back of my collar and physically pull me away. It was my lieutenant. He was trying to get me out of the immediate scene and obtain an initial briefing, but I had not even realized he was standing there.

He walked me back toward my patrol vehicle and asked whether I was okay. I gave him a quick explanation of what had happened. He told me it sounded like I had acted appropriately and within policy. Then he asked how many rounds I thought I had fired I told him,

"Three or four."

He replied,

"Based on the amount of brass I just walked past, I don't think that's accurate."

He was right.

I later learned I had fired fifteen rounds and struck the suspect thirteen times. The distance was approximately 136 feet. I also later learned that the victim's wound was unsurvivable. The round entered above her right hip, ricocheted off her pelvic bone upward through her chest cavity, and severed both her aorta and vena cava. Even if she had been lying in an operating room when it happened, survival would have been unlikely.

Beyond the physical destruction, one of my worst professional nightmares had occurred. I had witnessed a murder and then committed a justifiable homicide. Two lives were permanently lost, and nothing could undo that. The motive was jealousy. The ex-boyfriend had been drinking throughout the night, armed himself, and gone to confront the victim over the end of their relationship. From the moment I arrived on scene to the conclusion of the incident, less than four minutes had passed. I had always been taught that domestic violence calls and traffic stops are among the most dangerous situations in law enforcement.

That call proved it.

To this day, I still think about the victim's daughter. I still wish there had been something or anything I could have done differently. But the reality is, there was not. I responded as quickly as possible, made sound tactical decisions, and acted immediately when a lethal threat appeared. That truth does not change the outcome.

Two people died.

A daughter lost her mother.

That daughter will carry that memory for the rest of her life. No parent should have to bury a child and no child should ever have to watch a parent die violently in front of them.

There are many lessons embedded in that incident, each one worthy of serious reflection. The first is that time in these situations moves differently than most people expect. From the outside, people often imagine officers arriving, setting up positions, discussing options, and gradually bringing a situation under control. This perception largely comes from what they see on television. In this case, from the moment I parked my patrol vehicle to the moment the suspect was on the ground, was only four minutes. In that span of time, decisions had to be made instantly, without hesitation and without perfect information. I had to make a decision on life or death in a matter of seconds, the same decisions that juries deliberate on for hours or even days. If I would have hesitated or took the time to have an internal moral debate, the suspect could have killed my partner and even the woman's daughter.

Training exists for exactly those moments. When the brain has only seconds to process what is happening, there is no time to debate tactics or search for answers. You fall back on what you have practiced. Every drill, every scenario, every repetition matters because those habits become the framework that supports your decision-making when adrenaline takes over.

The second lesson is that violence often unfolds without warning and without mercy. The suspect did not hesitate when he stepped out from behind those parked cars. He did not negotiate, argue, or threaten first. He simply raised his weapon and fired. In that moment, there were no good outcomes left to choose from, only the least catastrophic one.

The third lesson is one that officers struggle with long after incidents like this are over: the weight of what cannot be changed. Even when every decision is legally justified and tactically sound, the human consequences remain. A daughter lost her mother. A man lost his life. Families were shattered in seconds, and nothing anyone could say or do would ever undo that.

People often assume that when an officer survives a lethal encounter, the story ends there. In reality, that is only the beginning of a different kind of struggle. Investigations begin. Statements are taken. Reports are written. Administrators review every detail of what happened. Media coverage appears. Questions are asked repeatedly by people who were not present and who will never fully understand the conditions under which those decisions were made.

Then there is the internal weight, the quiet moments afterward when the scene replays itself in your mind.

Could you have arrived faster?

Could you have positioned differently?

Could something have changed the outcome?

These questions are natural, but they rarely have satisfying answers. In my case, the facts were clear. The suspect fired first. The threat was immediate. My response stopped him from firing again. The investigation ultimately concluded that my actions were justified and within policy. However, justification does not erase memory. It does not erase the image of a daughter screaming beside her mother in the street. It does not erase the smell of gunpowder hanging in the air. It does not erase the knowledge that two lives ended in a matter of seconds.

Law enforcement officers carry moments like this with them for the rest of their careers. Some carry them longer. It is part of the burden of responding to other people's worst moments. The public often sees only the headlines or the brief description of events. What they rarely see is the quiet aftermath, the reflection, the responsibility, and the emotional cost that follows.

Another important lesson from that morning is the value of preparation. The decision to deploy a rifle before arriving on scene was not dramatic or heroic. It was simply a tactical decision based on the information available at the time. Had that rifle not been in my hands, the situation may have unfolded very differently. Equipment, training, and mindset matter long before the first shot is ever fired.

Finally, the incident reinforced something every experienced officer eventually learns: control is often an illusion. We can prepare, train, and think through scenarios, but the world does not follow a script. Calls develop unpredictably. People make irrational decisions. Violence erupts in places that seemed peaceful only minutes before. What we can control is our preparation, our discipline, and our commitment to doing the right thing when the moment arrives.

That morning reminded me that law enforcement is not defined by routine calls or quiet shifts. It is defined by the rare moments when everything changes in seconds and the decisions made in those seconds carry consequences that last forever.

Those moments are what officers train for.

Below are some important things to take away from this event;

- **Parking and Approach:**
  Where you park matters. Consider distance, angles of approach, available cover, lighting, and potential crossfire. Your patrol vehicle should not become a target or trap before the call even begins.

- **Equipment Selection:**

  Decide early what tools you may need. Patrol rifle, medical gear, extra magazines, and lighting. These decisions should be made before contact, not after the threat presents itself.

- **Pre-Arrival Scene Assessment:**

  Use all available information from dispatch and prior calls to form a working plan. Evaluate the location, time of day, known occupants, and past interactions. Mental preparation before arrival often dictates physical performance once on scene.

- **Physiological Stress Response:**

  It is widely known that when heart rate exceeds approximately 180 beats per minute, the body enters fight-or-flight. Tunnel vision, auditory exclusion, and loss of fine motor skills are common. Training under elevated heart rate conditions is essential so your body knows how to function when your mind is overloaded.

- **Weapon Manipulation Under Stress:** Simple tasks become difficult under stress reloading, holstering and unholstering, shouldering a rifle, and acquiring a sight picture. These skills must be ingrained through repetition and stress exposure, not assumed.

- **Round Accountability:** Be deliberate with every round sent downrange. Shot placement matters. Every round fired counts in a critical incident, and you are responsible for each one intended target or not.

- **Post-Incident Scene Management:** Once the immediate threat is neutralized, the incident is not over. Secure weapons, assess for additional threats, identify victims, and prepare for the next phase of a critical incident response.

- **First Aid and Medical Response:** Transition quickly from force to care. Rendering aid when safe to do so is not only a duty but often the difference between life and death.

- **The Quiet After:**
  Prepare for the silence that follows. The adrenaline drops, the emotional weight, and the mental replay are real. Understanding this phase and seeking support when needed is part of surviving a critical incident, not a sign of weakness.

XV

You're Never Out of the Fight

There is a moment in this profession when you realize the fight does not always look the way you expected it to. It is not always fists, gunfire, or flashing lights. Sometimes the fight is quieter. Sometimes it is internal and sometimes it begins only after the sirens stop and everyone else has gone home.

Law enforcement has a way of teaching you that the fight never truly ends it simply changes form. Early in my career, I believed the fight existed only on the street. It was measured in calls answered, suspects detained, and shifts survived. If I made it home at the end of the night, I believed I had won.

The job has a way of correcting that belief.

Survival and success are not the same thing. Making it through a shift does not mean you walk away untouched by it. The truth is, you are never completely out of the fight. Not when the call clears. Not when the paperwork is finished. Not even when the uniform comes off. The fight follows you home. It shows up in restless sleep, in short tempers, and in moments when silence feels heavier than noise. It lives in memories you never asked to keep and scenes that replay long after they should have faded.

Every call leaves a mark. Some are small and fade quickly. Others sink deep and stay. Over time, you begin carrying a collection of moments faces you could not save, decisions you replay in your head, words you wish you could take back or say one more time. The public rarely sees this part of the job. But it is the part officers carry the longest.

Some fights arrive without warning. There is the fight to stay patient when cynicism begins creeping in. The fight to remain compassionate after seeing the worst humanity has to offer. The fight to keep your sense of humor without letting it harden into cruelty. None of these battles are covered in academy manuals. Each one tests you in ways you were never fully warned about.

Then there is the fight within yourself. The doubt that whispers you could have done more. The guilt that asks why someone else did not make it home. The fear that one bad decision could define your entire career. These battles do not come over the radio and they come quietly. Unfortunately, more often than not, they demand to be faced alone.

That is why mental health cannot be treated as an afterthought in this profession. It has to be part of the fight plan.

Being proactive means acknowledging the impact of the job before it becomes overwhelming. It means treating mental health with the same seriousness as physical fitness, firearms training, and officer safety.

Simple actions matter more than people realize. Talk to someone you trust before things pile up. Check in on your partners and allow them to check in on you. Professional help is not a sign of weakness; it is a tool. Peer support teams, therapists who specialize in working with first responders, chaplains, and employee assistance programs exist for a reason. Using those resources does not mean you are broken. It means you are maintaining yourself so you can continue to serve and live well.

You also have to create space outside the badge. Sleep, exercise, and nutrition are not luxuries, they are necessities. When the body is neglected, the mind follows quickly behind. Hobbies, faith, family, fitness, and friendships that have nothing to do with law enforcement provide balance. They remind you that you are more than your worst call or your hardest shift. The badge may define your responsibilities, but the badge should never define your entire identity.

One of the hardest battles officers face is learning that strength does not mean silence. Law enforcement culture has long rewarded endurance over expression. But real strength is knowing when to speak up, when to ask for help, and when to say, *"That one affected me."* That fight takes courage and the fight is ongoing. Over the years, I have watched officers get knocked down physically, emotionally, and professionally and stand back up anyway. I have seen people question themselves, rebuild their confidence, and return stronger than before. Being knocked down does not mean you are out of the fight.

It means the fight has changed.

The battle extends beyond the job itself. It is the effort to be present with your family after carrying other people's trauma all day. It is learning how to leave work at work when your mind refuses to cooperate. It is figuring out who you are when the badge is no longer the easiest answer. Even retirement does not end the fight. It simply shifts again, like it has many times during the course of your career.

You fight to reconnect with a world that kept moving while you stood watch. You fight to make peace with the things you saw and the decisions you made. You fight to remember that your value was never tied solely to a uniform.

But there is hope in that truth.

If you are never completely out of the fight, then **you are never without purpose**. Every day offers another chance to choose integrity, to show compassion, and to take care of yourself and the people beside you. The fight is not always loud, sometimes it is simply choosing to keep going, and choosing to take care of your mind along the way.

May these lessons on Service, Sacrifice, and Survival help pave the way to a long and successful career.

This is the Cost of the Badge

You are never out of the fight.

Conclusion:

This book was never meant to be a victory lap or a collection of war stories. It was written as a training tool; one I wish I had when I first put on the badge. Every lesson, mistake, and hard truth shared here exists for one reason: so, others can learn without paying the same price.

The lessons in this book were not learned in a classroom. They were earned under stress, through failure, and sometimes at significant cost. Growth in this profession does not come from pretending we are flawless. It comes from accountability, reflection, and the willingness to improve.

Law enforcement will test your integrity, judgment, and resilience. It will place you in moments that cannot be undone and decisions that stay with you for a lifetime. The goal is not perfection, it is preparation. Train harder than required. Learn beyond what is offered. Choose mentors carefully. Protect your integrity relentlessly.

If you are early in your career, I hope this helps you avoid mistakes that could derail your future. If you are experienced, I hope it serves as a reminder that growth never stops. At some point, the radio goes silent, the calls stop, and the uniform comes off. The structure and urgency that once defined your life is gone, but the perspective remains. You still notice what others miss. You still carry the experiences, decisions, and moments that shaped you. The badge may come off, but its impact does not.

When the pace slows, space is created. In that space, things you pushed aside like memories, faces, and moments you never fully processed can resurface. This is not weakness. It is the result of carrying more than most people ever will. During the job, you had somewhere to place that weight. After the job, you have to learn how to face it, sometimes alone.

That takes intention.

It means acknowledging what you have been through. It means talking to someone you trust. It means understanding that handling something in the moment does not mean it had no lasting effect. Taking care of your mental health is not about fixing something broken. It is about maintaining something that has been tested.

If you are not in law enforcement and are reading this, there is still something here for you. You may never face the situations described in this book, but you will face moments that require judgment, discipline, and responsibility. At times, others will look to you for direction.

The principles are the same.

Be disciplined, think before you act, and learn continuously. Take ownership of your decisions and when the moment comes that requires you to step forward, do so with intention. At some point, in your own way, you will face a real problem. How you respond will matter.

For those who have worn the badge, the question always comes:

Was it worth it?

There is no perfect answer. The cost is real, missed time, strained relationships, and moments that never leave. But so is the meaning. You remember the quiet calls and the times things did not get worse because you were there. You also remember the moments where you stood between chaos, control, and held the line. The badge was never about power. It was about the responsibility to step forward when others stepped back.

It was never about what you got from the badge. It was about what you were willing to give.

Acknowledgments:

This book would not exist without the steady presence of those who stood beside me; sometimes quietly, sometimes firmly, through both the best and most difficult moments of my career. While law enforcement is often portrayed as an individual profession, the reality is that no one endures it alone. Every lesson captured in these pages was shaped by conversations, shared experiences, hard-earned corrections, and the unwavering support of others.

To my family, thank you for your patience, understanding, and the sacrifices made behind the scenes, often without recognition, but never without impact. Your support provided the foundation that made everything else possible.

To my partners, thank you for your trust, your vigilance, and your willingness to stand shoulder to shoulder in moments that demanded clarity, courage, and accountability. The lessons learned together, both spoken and unspoken, are woven throughout these pages.

To my mentors, thank you for your guidance, your standards, and your willingness to correct when it mattered most. Your influence shaped not only how I approached the profession, but how I continue to grow within it.

To the man who taught me how to study with purpose, approach tests with confidence, carry myself with assurance and humility, thank you. I am profoundly grateful for the role you have played in my journey. Without your guidance, I would not have achieved the milestones I have reached nor experienced the success I am fortunate to hold today.

Every award, accolade, and achievement I have earned is a reflection of your influence and belief in me. Your selflessness and unwavering commitment to going above and beyond have never gone unnoticed. You believed in me when I could not yet believe in myself, and for that, I am forever thankful.

I am deeply appreciative of the potential you saw in me and for the way you challenged and strengthened me, truly embodying the principle that iron sharpens iron.

These acknowledgments are not offered as mere formalities, but as a sincere expression of gratitude for the patience, guidance, accountability, and belief extended to me over the years. I was taught through instruction, through example, and at times through difficult lessons that required growth and reflection.

To all who contributed in ways both seen and unseen, thank you.

www.ingramcontent.com/pod-product-compliance
Lightning Source LLC
LaVergne TN
LVHW090613110826
845146LV00001B/374

* 9 7 9 8 9 9 5 6 3 1 8 0 4 *